CliffsNotes®

Graduation Debt

2nd Edition

How to Manage Student Loans and Live Your Life

by Reyna Gobel, M.B.A., M.J.

Houghton Mifflin Harcourt
Boston • New York

CliffsNotes® Graduation Debt, 2nd Edition

Copyright © 2014 by Houghton Mifflin Harcourt Publishing Company

All rights reserved.

Cover illustration by Richard Weiss © Images.com/Corbis

Library of Congress Control Number: 2013950711

ISBN: 978-0-544-31909-7 (pbk)

Printed in the United States of America

DOC 10 9 8 7 6 5 4 3 2 1

For information about permission to reproduce selections from this book, write to
Permissions, Houghton Mifflin Harcourt Publishing Company, 215 Park Avenue South,
New York, New York 10003.

www.hmhco.com

Peggy Engel, Dr. James Conover,
Grace Freedson, Jeff Inman, and my
mom and dad, Caryl and Ed Gobel.
Without any of these people, this
book wouldn't have happened.

Acknowledgments

Thank you:

Peggy Engel, my mentor, for believing a book on repaying student loans needed to be written, and that I was the one who should write it.

Grace Freedson, my literary agent, for sticking by a first-time book author through fruition.

Greg Tubach and the rest of the gang at Houghton Mifflin Harcourt for giving me the honor of writing under the CliffsNotes brand. Lori Glazer, Katrina Kruse, and Alison Klooster for helping me get the word out that this book exists. And, of course, my editor, Christina Stambaugh, who kept my writing and timing on track when I started to go off on tangents.

My interviewees, who agreed to talk conversationally about their subject of expertise: Tom Harnisch, Barry Paperno, Robbi Ernst III, Martha Holler, Patricia Christel, Debby Hohler, Jim Southwell, Sarah Kaufman, Jacqueline Fairbairn, Bob Meighan, Teri Gault, Tony Bambacino, and Dr. James Conover.

My real-life interviewees, who trusted me enough to share their debt stories: Dawn, Melissa, and Kristen and Erik.

All the editors who let a former and still occasional entertainment and pop culture writer near the subject of education, especially Allison Gualtieri, Paula Kashtan, and Will Chen. My marketing manager, Irene Mitchell, who books my speeches so I can help the maximum number of people deal with their student loans.

My mom and dad, who taught me to find a way to help others, and to do math problems without a calculator.

My friends, who support me in everything that I do, including tolerating me talking endlessly about student loans and personal finance: Kati Ianello, Liz Dwelle, Camille Jensen, Sona Charaipatra, Michele Wojciechowski, Marla Backman, Beverly Harzog, Allie Johnson, Jeff and Gus, Dan Grodzian, and Rabbi Simcha.

All the kids in my life who provide smiles and inspiration: David, Jade, Abbi, Edie, Eddie, Grace, Claire, and Kavya.

Jane Glickman, for her invaluable research help on student loan regulations.

My first writing mentor, Jeff Inman, who was the first person who taught me how to write well.

Finally, I'd like to thank Brooklyn for being such an amazing place to live and work as a writer. When I want to leave my home to be around people while I write, there's never a shortage of writer-friendly cafés that let me work for hours while ordering one cup of coffee.

Table of Contents

About the Author

Reyna Gobel, M.B.A. and M.J., is a freelance journalist who specializes in financial fitness. Her financial advice appears regularly on www.investopedia.com and Yahoo!Finance, as well as other print and online outlets.

Introduction

When you started college, student loans may have seemed like a gift to help you get through school. However, your gift was borrowed money. I knew my student loans were borrowed money, but I never thought about how I was going to pay them back. I assumed that when I got a grown-up job, the money I made would easily allow me to make the payments every month without affecting my lifestyle. The debt crept up on me, one semester's worth of loans at a time. Some semesters my loans totaled around $1,000; other semesters they totaled over $7,000. After a bachelor's degree and two master's degrees, I racked up $63,000 in student loan debt. Even though it was consolidated at a low 4 percent interest rate, it will still take 30 years to pay off, at $310 a month.

Those of us with mountains of student loan debt are not alone. Based on data from the National Center for Education Statistics, there are over one million graduates who have at least $40,000 in student loan debt in the United States alone.

If everyone in this predicament who has 25- and 30-year loan terms waited until these debts were paid off to start families, save for retirement, or move out of their first apartments, no one would ever leave their matchbox-sized apartment or get married!

But most of us are not going to wait until middle age to start living our lives, nor should we. Since we are going to have our student debt around for up to 30 years, we need to learn to manage our payments as another bill we have to pay, similar to an electric bill or a rent payment. You can manage your student debt while maintaining a lifestyle that is productive in the grand scheme of a financially secure future.

By the end of this book, you will learn how to find loans for semesters you have long forgotten, and devise a plan to make payments and eventually pay off your educational loans. You'll learn when and how to use options for postponing your loans when you have temporary financial difficulties, such as a layoff or reduced or no pay during maternity leave.

You will also learn how to discuss debt with your significant other, manage your other debts, keep your head above water during periods of inflation and recession, rebuild your credit rating, and still enjoy most of your guilty pleasures while you reform your budget.

I can't promise that you will have your student debt paid off by the time you finish this book—unless you take ten years to read it. But, by the end of this book, you will have a plan in place that will help you deal with your student debt and manage your financial life without feeling like your debt will be a hindrance to what you want to accomplish.

Evaluating Your Student Debt Situation

If you pay your student loan bills every month, and then try to forget the giant pile of debt to which your loans are attached—stop! In order to work toward paying off your student loan debt, you need to be aware of the existence and the amounts of each loan.

You no longer should think about whether you borrowed too much, or if you should have rejected the part of your student loan you used for spring break. Your new focus is on making small changes to pay off your loans faster without impacting your life. The first step on this path is looking up the specifics of all your federal loans in the National Student Loan Data System.

Facing Your Student Debt Demons

Where do you begin when it comes to dealing with your debt? Figure out what your starting point is by taking the following pop quiz to find out how much you really know about your student loans. If you don't know some of the answers, don't worry. This quiz comes with instructions for creating a kind of "cheat sheet" for getting the details on your loans.

1. How many different federal student loans do you have? _____

   (You could have two or more per semester you were in school, and don't forget loans for graduate school or for any community college or summer courses at other universities.)

2. Are they all consolidated into one loan? ___ yes ___ no

3. How many are subsidized? _____

4. How many are unsubsidized? _____

5. Who are the servicers on each student loan? (Use an additional sheet of paper if you have more servicers than can fit in the spaces provided.)

_____

_____

_____

_____

_____

_____

_____

6. Do you have the contact information in a file? ___ yes   ___ no

7. Do you know where the file is? ___ yes   ___ no

8. Do you know your interest rates on every single loan?

___ yes   ___ no

9. If you put one loan in forbearance or deferment—temporary hold on making payments—did you remember to hold others?

___ yes   ___ no

How did you do? If you didn't know all the answers, you are not alone. Whether you just graduated from college or you've been out of school for a decade, it's not always easy to keep tabs on eight semesters of loans—or more if you went to grad school or took five or six years to graduate—when each could be with a separate servicer. Luckily, the federal government offers a free Web site (www.nslds.ed.gov) where you can locate all of your federal loans, what servicer they are with, and the details of how much you owe. By accessing this information you can build a kind of cheat sheet to help keep track of your loans.

The National Student Loan Data System (NSLDS)

With the information in the National Student Loan Data System, you can find out your interest rates and get copies of your loan contracts by calling and requesting the necessary information from your current servicers with the phone numbers provided within your financial aid review.

Using the National Student Loan Data System Web site will involve taking the following steps.

FIND YOUR PIN

The National Student Loan Data System requires a PIN (personal identification number) to access your federal student loan information. You have a PIN to access your student loan information for the same reason you have one to access your bank or credit card information. You have an account with the federal government and/or accounts with the lenders backed by the federal government. What's contained in the Student Loan Data System is a large part of your student loan information.

If you received aid since the beginning of electronic financial aid applications, you created a PIN for retrieving your FAFSA (Free Application for Student Aid) that was your first step in getting federal loans to attend college.

The best way to get started on finding your loan information is getting or recovering your PIN at the PIN Web site: https://pin.ed.gov/PINWebApp/appinstr.jsp. If you've used your PIN in the last 18 months to check on your student loans and you still remember it, you have all the information you need to log in to the National Student Loan Data System. You can jump to the next section of this chapter.

If you don't remember your PIN and you have used it in the last 18 months, you have to go to the PIN Web site: www.pin.ed.gov, which you can use to generate a PIN or retrieve your PIN. You will have to answer a question based on information you provided on your FAFSA for security. For example, if you selected "What is your mother's maiden name?" as your challenge question when you received your PIN, you would need to provide your mother's maiden name in order to get a duplicate PIN.

If you don't have one, you can create a 4-digit PIN at https://pin.ed.gov/PINWebApp/appinstr.jsp. You will need to provide your Social Security number, full name, address, e-mail address, and security question (a question about yourself for security purposes). Select a question that you can always answer and spell the same, such as your mother's maiden name, the name of your elementary school, or the name of the hospital you were born in. But you still want to be careful about capitalization and abbreviations. The PIN Web site is case sensitive. Also, don't fill in an answer that you sometimes abbreviate. For example, if your challenge question is "What is the name of your high school?"

and you attended Century High School, you won't be able to access your account if you type in CHS.

Name changes will not affect your PIN for all of your previous loans. Your PIN is attached to the name you had when you borrowed the money. However, if you return to college, you need to create a new PIN under your new legal name.

Checklist for Finding Your Student Loan PIN

✓ Remember that your student loan PIN is the same PIN you used when you filled out your FAFSA when applying for student aid. Now, it is the number that identifies you for retrieving all your federal student loan information.

✓ If you don't have your PIN, you can request a new one at the PIN Web site: www.pin.ed.gov.

✓ Use the last name you had when you were in college with your PIN.

✓ You will need to request a new PIN if you haven't used your PIN for applying for student loans or retrieving your student loan information in the last 18 months.

ACCESS THE NATIONAL STUDENT LOAN DATA SYSTEM WEB SITE

Now that you have your PIN, you can sign in to the National Student Loan Data System Web site at www.nslds.ed.gov. Brace yourself, because you are going to see how much interest has accrued since the first day you borrowed your first student loan dollar. How high could that number be? Let's say you borrowed $3,400 in the spring semester of 2004 with an average interest rate of 5 percent. If you haven't paid a nickel on that loan by November 2013, you will have accrued $1,638 in interest, bringing your total owed to $5,038.

From the NSLDS home page, click on Financial Aid Review. Accept the terms and enter your Social Security number, the first two letters of your last name during college, your date of birth, and your PIN. The first page you will see is a chart displaying a list of your loans with Type of Loan, Loan Amount, Loan Date, Disbursed Amount, Canceled Amount, Outstanding Principal, and Outstanding Interest. What do all these terms mean and how is this chart going to help you manage your loans?

The chart on the student loan data system Web site will give you all the information you need to find your student loans and information about them. However, if the chart just looks like a bunch of gibberish with the dozens of terms you need to know, you won't get much out of it. So let's look first at an explanation of the terms that will be most important in deciphering the information you need.

Types of Loans

The federal government categorizes your loans in several different ways:

- **Consolidated:** This is a combined loan from multiple semesters. For example, if you consolidated loans after you finished your undergraduate degree, you could have eight semesters of loans in one consolidation loan.

- **Subsidized:** With a subsidized loan, the government pays your interest while you attend college and other special circumstances.

- **Unsubsidized:** With an unsubsidized loan, you pay your own interest in all circumstances.

> ### Caution
>
> If you consolidated your loans after graduation, it doesn't mean all of your loans were consolidated. If you forget to name a loan to your servicer, it may have fallen by the wayside. When you construct your Personal Student Loan chart at the end of this chapter, look at the balances owed on all your loans, whether or not you believe it was consolidated.

- **FFEL (Federal Family Education Loan) Program:** These loans are with a servicer other than the government but they are federally backed loans and qualify for most of the same repayment programs as direct loans. They can also be consolidated to direct lending.

- **Direct:** This kind of loan is issued directly from the government via direct lending as a servicer.

- **Stafford:** The most common type of federal loan, it can come in many forms, such as consolidated or unconsolidated or subsidized or unsubsidized. It can be serviced by either direct lending or another servicer.

- **Perkins:** This category of student loans is fairly rare and is normally reserved for low-income families. If you have these, you may have additional options for loan forgiveness.

Loans Chart Categories

Not sure what all the terms mean on your Loans chart? Use the following term list as a guideline for the categories you'll see:

- **Loan Amount:** The amount you were approved to borrow for a specific semester. This amount may not have the amount you received. For instance, let's say you were approved for $6,000, but you decided you only needed $3,500. The other $2,500 you were approved for you don't have to pay back because you never borrowed this money.

- **Loan Date:** This is the date you originally took out your loan. It is helpful in deciphering in which semester you borrowed that particular amount of money. Be aware that you could have more than one loan per semester. For instance, let's say the government gave you *x* amount of money in a certain semester in a subsidized loan where your interest is paid while you attend college. Then you were given an additional loan to cover the rest of your expenses in the form of an unsubsidized loan.

- **Disbursed Amount:** This is the original amount of money you borrowed on the specified loan date. It has nothing to do with how much you owe now, because interest has accrued and payments have been made. For example, in the fall semester of 2003, you borrowed a student loan in the amount of $3,500. After seven years of an average interest rate of 5 percent, you now owe $4,924 (figuring in compounded interest).

- **Canceled Amount:** If you see a canceled amount on your Loans chart, it means that amount is no longer owed. It could be for a variety of reasons: Perhaps you became disabled and could no longer make payments, you completed a loan forgiveness program, or you rejected part of the financial aid package you were rewarded. For example, I applied for financial aid in my last semester of school. However, I looked at the debt I'd already accumulated and decided I didn't want to have $70,000 worth of student loan debt. So I arranged a payment plan with my university to pay over the course of the semester instead of taking on new debt. For that particular semester, a cancelled amount is shown on my Loans chart for the loans I turned down.

- **Outstanding Principal:** This is the amount of your original loan that you still owe. However, outstanding interest is added to this amount to create your total balance. For example, let's say you consolidated all your loans into one 30-year loan of $60,000 in 2011. You've been making payments for two years and have an interest rate of 5 percent. You now owe $58,184. This reflects $1,816 you've paid toward your principal, but it doesn't have anything to do with the $5,915 you've already spent in interest.

- **Enrollment Status:** Your enrollment status dictates whether you are a part-time student, full-time student, graduate student, or have graduated. Although your enrollment status won't affect anything in the Student Loan chart you will create at the end of this chapter, it could affect consolidation if you are still in school (see Chapter 3, "Consolidating Your Federal Loans"). Generally, you will wait until after graduation to consolidate your loans.

- **Outstanding Interest:** The outstanding interest is the interest accrued since your last student loan payment. This could be what has accrued during a period of temporary payment reprieve or since your last monthly payment.

- **Repayment:** When you start sending in your loans, you'll start to hear the term repayment constantly. This just means that you are repaying your loan company for the payments you received when you were in college.

> **Caution**
>
> Don't get thrown off if the aid summary shows your new name at the top. You still log in under your former legal name if you are using your original PIN number.

Checklist for Understanding Student Loan Terms

- ✓ Print your charts from the National Student Loan Data System.
- ✓ Go through the information in your charts and make a list of the terms you don't know.
- ✓ Look up those terms in the Types of Loans and Loans Chart Categories lists in this chapter.
- ✓ Refer to the lists if you have questions as you get further into organizing your debt.

FIND ALL OF YOUR STUDENT LOANS

When you look at your first chart on the opening page of your file on the National Student Loan Data System Web site, you see information that you never knew existed about your student loans in terms you don't normally think about, such as cancelled amounts and disbursed amounts. So it's hard to know where you should start in order to figure out which loans you still have balances on and how much you currently owe.

Take it one chart at a time, beginning with your Loans chart. This chart is on your personal home page after you successfully log in to the National Student Loan Data System. All your loans are listed in order from your newest to your oldest. Thus, if you've consolidated your loans into one or two spiffy new loans with one convenient payment, these will more likely be numbers 1 and 2—unless you received more loans after you consolidated your loans into one loan. For example, if you went back to school for a graduate degree and went a little deeper into student loan debt, these loans would be newer than your consolidation loans.

The reason why you could see two consolidation loans instead of one is because consolidated loans are separated into subsidized and unsubsidized loans. This is in case you return to school or otherwise qualify for a temporary loan deferment—a reprieve from making payments in which the government pays your interest on the subsidized portion of your loan. This doesn't mean that if you have all your loans consolidated with the same company that you won't make one payment. Your loan company divides the payment for you between the loans so you only have to think about making one payment.

Now that you know the organization, scan through your loans and look for the loans in which you still have balances. Keep in mind that any of the loans you consolidated into one larger loan will show a $0 balance. Take a look at the sample chart for Johnny Debt on pages 10–11, a fictitious person who borrowed nearly $60,000 in student debt. He will be used in this chapter as a step-by-step example of how you can gather information from the charts on the National Student Loan Data System and create your own Personal Student Loan chart with the information you need to organize your student debt.

On the sample Loans chart on pages 10–11, you'll see that Johnny Debt has $0 balances for loans in the Outstanding Principal column for loans 3 through 10 and loans 12 through 16.

At this point, you should print a copy of your own Loans chart and highlight the loans that have balances in the Outstanding Principal column. You can figure out how much you owe on each loan by adding your outstanding principal with your outstanding interest owed.

Caution

Outstanding interest doesn't have anything to do with the total amount you paid in interest. This is only the interest that has recently built onto your loan—usually since your last payment.

Checklist for Understanding Your Loans Chart

✓ Log on to the National Student Loan Data System to view your Loans chart.

✓ Print out your chart and highlight which loans you still have balances on based on seeing an owed amount in your Outstanding Principal column.

✓ Carefully scan your chart for loans you may have missed in consolidation or forgotten about, and highlight those loans as well.

Making Sense of Your Individual Charts

If you just viewed your Loans chart and were pleasantly surprised that there were no surprises about your loans, give yourself a big pat on the back for a job well done. You can peruse this section casually while sitting back in your chair without having to pay too much attention to the checklist. However, I still want you to have your pen handy to fill out the chart in the next section, because constructing this chart will be important for future chapters and possibly finding better or cheaper student loan repayment options.

On the other hand, if your loans did have some surprises, click on the numbers of those and you'll see charts similar to the ones Johnny Debt has.

AMOUNTS AND DATES

In the Amounts and Dates chart, the dates don't have to do with when you first took out your loan. Instead, the dates tell you what date the interest and principal amounts are based on. For instance, if you just made a payment on February 10 and the interest and principal dates are January 31, you know that your interest and principal amounts are a little lower than reported on the chart. If you had part of your loan cancelled, the date of cancellation is also shown.

While this chart doesn't show your actual interest rate, it does show whether your rate is fixed or variable. In 2006, all student loans started being issued with fixed rates, but any loans you have before July 1, 2006, that aren't consolidated will have variable rates that are set annually on July 1. In Johnny Debt's case, I chose to select his number 11 loan from his chart to learn about. This is because he forgot to include this loan in his consolidation, so he needs to know the details of its current status.

	Type of Loan	Loan Amount	Loan Date
	Johnny Debt's Loans Chart		
1	FFEL Consolidated	$12,001	7/1/2004
2	FFEL Consolidated	$15,375	7/1/2004
3	Stafford Subsidized	$2,750	2/1/2001
4	Stafford Unsubsidized	$2,500	2/1/2001
5	Stafford Subsidized	$2,750	9/1/2000
6	Stafford Unsubsidized	$2,500	9/1/2000
7	Stafford Subsidized	$2,750	2/1/2000
8	Stafford Unsubsidized	$2,500	2/1/2000
9	Stafford Subsidized	$2,750	9/1/1999
10	Stafford Unsubsidized	$2,500	9/1/1999
11	Stafford Subsidized	$1,750	2/1/1999
12	Stafford Unsubsidized	$2,000	2/1/1999
13	Stafford Subsidized	$1,750	9/1/1998
14	Stafford Unsubsidized	$2,000	9/1/1998
15	Direct Stafford Subsidized	$1,225	2/1/1998
16	Direct Stafford Subsidized	$1,400	9/1/1997
	Total FFEL Consolidated		
	Total Stafford Subsidized		
	Total Stafford Unsubsidized		
	Total All Loans		

Disbursed Amount	Canceled Amount	Outstanding Principal	Outstanding Interest
$12,001	$0	$8,210.03	$17
$15,375	$0	$10,518.22	$22
$2,750	$0	$0	$0
$2,500	$0	$0	$0
$2,750	$0	$0	$0
$2,500	$0	$0	$0
$2,750	$0	$0	$0
$2,500	$0	$0	$0
$2,750	$0	$0	$0
$2,500	$0	$0	$0
$1,750	$0	$1,825.80	$804.33
$2,000	$0	$0	$0
$1,750	$0	$0	$0
$2,000	$0	$0	$0
$1,225	$0	$0	$0
$1,400	$0	$0	$0
		$18,728.25	$39
		$1,825.80	$804.33
		$0	$0
		$20,554.05	$843.33

Johnny Debt's Amounts and Dates Chart		
Loan Amount	Outstanding Principal Balance	Outstanding Principal Balance as of Date
$1,750	$1,825.80	3/10/13

Johnny Debt's Disbursement(s) and Status(es) Chart		
Disbursement Date	Disbursement Amount	Loan Status
2/1/1999	$1,750	XD
		RP
		IF

In the preceding sample Amounts and Dates chart, you can see that Johnny Debt has a variable interest rate. This shows that the loan was not included in his consolidation loan, because once you consolidate your loan, your loan is always at a fixed rate. We also know from the chart that the outstanding principal and interest on the loan is up to date as of March 10, 2013.

DISBURSEMENT(S) AND STATUS(ES)

The Disbursement(s) and Status(es) chart is an important one if you don't know what has happened to your student loan. The status description box lets you see what's going on with your student debt, from the date your loan was issued to present day. You can also see on what dates the status changed, so if your loan went astray, you will know exactly when it happened.

Johnny Debt definitely has a wayward loan. As you can see from the following sample Disbursement(s) and Status(es) chart, his loan is presently in default, which is the term used to describe a loan that has not had payments made on it for an extended period of time. It is looked at on your credit report similar to a charge-off, but it has much worse consequences because student loan debt cannot be expunged in bankruptcy. (Please see Chapter 2, "Organizing Your Student Debt Payments," for more information on defaults.)

How did his loan end up in default? Johnny had great intentions. He paid all his other loans that he remembered on time and for a few months at a time received economic forbearances when needed. But in the middle of ten loans, he forgot this one in his consolidation. You

Outstanding Interest Balance	Interest Rate	Canceled Amount	Canceled Date
$804.33	Variable	$0	-

Status Description	Status Effective Date
Defaulted, six consecutive payments	6/10/2002
Repayment	11/10/2001
In school or grace period	2/1/1999

can see his status change in a year's time in the chart from in school because he was still in college to in repayment. Because he didn't make payments, after a number of months, he went into default.

If you have a loan in default, check out Chapter 2 for tips on how to rehab your loan.

SERVICER/LENDER/GUARANTY AGENCY INFORMATION

If you have a rogue loan—a loan you forgot about—the Servicer/ Lender/Guaranty Agency Information chart is important because you need to know who to contact. You can also use this information if you need the number for your servicer so you can call to ask questions about your interest rates, terms of your loan, your payment history, or the time left to finish paying off your loans.

The servicer is the company that handles customer service for the lender, and the one you are most in contact with. The guaranty company is the one who guarantees the loan for the lender. This is who you deal with once your loan has defaulted.

Johnny Debt needs to call his guaranty agency to make arrangements to rehabilitate his default and eventually get it back to repayment status. Not only did he not know the contact information, he had no idea who the servicer or lender was! This is because loans that aren't through direct lending can be sold and transferred by the lender. Just like if you had a mortgage through one bank and then the loan was sold to another, you would make your payments through the new bank and contact them with questions on your loan.

Checklist for Understanding Your Individual Charts

✓ Click on the number next to the loan you'd like information on to pull up charts on an individual loan.

✓ To find out if you have a variable- or fixed-rate loan, go to your Amounts and Dates chart and check the Interest Rate column.

✓ To find out the most recent status of your loan, go to your Disbursement(s) and Status(es) chart and look in the Status Description column that is located closest to the top of the column.

✓ To find contact information for your servicer, lender, or guaranty agency, go to your Servicer/Lender/Guaranty Agency Information chart.

> **Caution**
>
> If you have direct loans, you might still see a servicer listed that's not the federal government. This doesn't mean your loan is not a direct loan. It only means your loan is serviced by someone else. You still qualify for direct loan repayment options and programs.

Constructing Your Personal Student Loan Chart

By this point in the chapter, you may be experiencing chart overload. But I promise that this is the last one. I'm going to show you how to

Johnny Debt's Personal Student Loan Chart			
	Original Loan Date	Amount Owed	Current Servicer or Guaranty Agency
1	7/1/2004	$8,227.03	BANK C
2	7/1/2004	$10,540.22	BANK C
3	2/1/1999	$2,630.13	BANK A
Total FFEL consolidated loans		$18,767.25	
Total defaulted loans *		$2,630.13	
Total All Loans		**$21,397.38**	

*Does not include collection fees

combine all your student loan information that you just read about into one chart. Your Personal Student Loan chart will serve as a reference for your current student debt in future chapters. With your Personal Student Loan chart in front of you, you can evaluate repayment options and strategies for paying off your debt faster based on the debt you have.

Get out a piece of paper to construct the chart manually or open up a spreadsheet in your favorite computer program. You can also create a table in your favorite word processing program. No matter which method you choose, you'll use the following format.

In the rows, you'll list the loans for which you still owe balances. These are the ones you highlighted on your Loans chart after you printed it out. You'll assign each loan a number. Use the following as column titles:

- **Original Loan Date:** In this column you put the date you first borrowed your loan.

- **Amount Owed:** To find the amount you owe on an individual loan, add your outstanding principal with your outstanding interest.

- **Current Servicer:** The name of the servicer listed for this loan in the Servicer Lender/Guaranty Agency Information chart. (If you have a default, list the guaranty agency for this particular loan.)

Contact Information	Loan Type and Status	Interest Rate	Monthly Payment
(123) 555-4500	**FFEL CONSOLIDATED** unsubsidized In repayment	3.375%	$68.83
(123) 555-4500	**FFEL CONSOLIDATED** In repayment	3.375%	$88.19
(123) 555-4567	**STAFFORD UNSUBSIDIZED** defaulted	Variable	$200 on default rehabilitation payment plan
			$157.02
			$200
			$357.02

- **Contact Information:** The phone number listed for your servicer in the Servicer Lender/Guaranty Agency Information chart.

- **Loan Type and Status:** The information you need for this column is in your Loans chart under Type of Loan. The status is located in your Disbursement(s) and Status(es) chart under Status Description.

- **Interest Rate:** To find out what interest rate you are currently paying on your loan, contact your servicer. While you're at it, ask if your rate is fixed or variable. This will be important to know for loan repayment options, which I'll discuss in Chapters 2 and 3.

- **Monthly Payment:** Before you hang up with your servicer, find out what your current monthly payment is.

Check out the sample Personal Student Loan chart on pages 14–15 for an example of what it should look like when you're done. If you constructed your chart on your computer, print out a copy and keep it in a folder with exercises you'll complete in later chapters. If you filled in the chart on a piece of paper, keep it in a notebook, where you can also complete other exercises in later chapters.

Checklist for Chart Exercise

✓ Check your Loans chart to make sure you didn't forget any loans.

✓ Double-check the information on your Personal Student Loan chart with the information on your charts from the National Student Loan Data System.

✓ Click on the numbers for each loan you still have a balance on to view the individual loan charts and gather loan status and servicer contact information.

✓ Store your completed chart in a notebook or folder for easy reference.

Double Listings, Inaccurate Listings, and No Listings

Whether it's a double listing, no listing, or inaccurate listing, you will need to be proactive in correcting the problem. Each issue requires its own course of action.

DOUBLE LISTINGS

If you see a loan listed twice on your student loan reporting data, don't panic! If you've consolidated your loans, there might be one listing for the original loan, which you'll now see has a balance of 0. It could also be because your tuition was the same for both semesters of the same year and the original amounts are identical because you borrowed the same amount two semesters in a row.

However, like anything else, scrutinize this carefully and make sure you read the columns, and if you don't understand anything in your report, call the Department of Education. If there's something on there you don't understand, asking a question could mean the difference between progressing toward paying off your debt and missing a loan and going into default. How so? Let's say you have two loans for the same amount for different semesters. You only make payments on one loan or consolidate one because you confuse both for the same loan.

INACCURATE LISTINGS

You may notice a loan on your report that you thought you'd paid off—and you may have. Check your old bank statements for when the payment could have been taken out. If you don't have your old bank statements, call your bank and order them.

Just because you may have switched banks doesn't mean you can't find proof of your old payments. You can contact your former bank to gather old bank statements. Don't forget to check savings accounts or your parents' bank accounts that you may have made the payments out of as well.

Caution

Don't ignore anything on your report that doesn't look right. You could stop making payments on a loan that you actually owe money on and go into default. Check with the Department of Education and your servicer to correct any errors, especially if you see a loan you thought you paid off that shows an amount owed. Then call your bank to order a record of past bill payments, or cancelled checks for the payments if you are required to show proof of payments.

Once you find the information you need, contact your servicer and the Department of Education to correct the problem. Calling the servicer is of the utmost importance; a mistake may have occurred in their computer system where they are still reporting that you owe them money when you don't. Luckily, if you have your bank statements handy when you call them, you'll have the proof you need ready to send them so they can correct the errors.

No Listings

If you don't see a loan on your report when you know you did borrow the money, this can feel like a big birthday present. But it doesn't mean you should not take action. Check your records and your bank statements to verify that you did borrow this money. Contact both your servicer and the Department of Education about the error if you find there is one.

Checklist for Deciphering Double Listings, Inaccurate Listings, and No Listings

- ✓ Look for double listings based on same amount.
- ✓ Don't panic if you see a double listing. Most likely it is because you borrowed the same amount for two semesters in the same year.
- ✓ If you see a double listing, see if one shows a $0 balance. This could mean this loan was consolidated.
- ✓ Order past bank statements or cancelled checks as proof of your payments on no listings and inaccurate listings.
- ✓ Call the Department of Education and your servicer with remaining questions.
- ✓ Call your guaranty agency for details if your loan shows a default status.

Chapter Wrap-Up

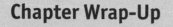

- $ You can't do anything about your student loans until you know how much total student debt you have, what the length of the repayment terms are, and what the loan's interest rate is. Make sure you have gathered all of your basic loan information on every loan you have.

- $ You can access all your federal student loan information on the National Student Loan Data System Web site: www.nslds.ed.gov.

- $ You will need the PIN you created when you first applied for your loans to access your data. If you forget your PIN, you can retrieve it at https://pin.ed.gov/PINWebApp/appinstr.jsp.

- $ If it's been more than 18 months since you've accessed your data or applied for a loan, you'll need to go to www.pin.ed.gov to apply for a new PIN.

- $ Keep all your student loan info in a manually written or computerized chart or table. Store Your Personal Student Loan chart in a place where you always know where it is. If you manually create your chart, keep it in a notebook where you can do other exercises from future chapters.

- $ There may be mistakes in your Loans chart. If you're in doubt, call the Department of Education and your loan's servicer.

- $ You can find the contact information for your loan servicers in the Servicer/Lender/Guaranty Agency Information chart.

- $ If a loan is missing from your National Student Loan Data System report, don't regard it as a gift. Double-check with the Department of Education and your servicer to see whether a mistake has been made.

Organizing Your Student Debt Payments

Whether you went to graduate school, medical school, or law school, organizing four years of student loans is hard. By the end of college, you could have two or three loans per semester for your bachelor's degree—totaling a whopping debt if you finished in four years instead of five or six. You could have even more loans if you went on to graduate school.

While organizing a mountain of debt might seem like an uphill battle, you have some advantages. Your federal student loans can be easily located if you forget one or two. You have more possible payment plans to make your loans affordable within your budget, options for temporary payment reprieves, and ways to recover financially from late or missed payments than nearly any other kind of loan.

Default Rehab

You were just turned down for a mortgage, and you don't understand why. You've maintained steady employment for the last five years, you pay all of your bills on time, and the required down payment is sitting in your bank account. When you ask the banker what happened, you are told you defaulted (failed to pay) on a student loan. It doesn't make sense to you because you're shelling out hundreds of dollars every month to your student loan servicers. What happened?

Odds are you forgot about one of your student loans and it went into default. This is fairly common. In a ten-year study conducted by the National Center for Education Statistics that followed the graduating class of 1993, 20 percent of those who had at least $15,000 in Stafford Loans had defaulted on at least one of their education loans. Others, including myself, thought they were making payments on all their loans but misplaced information on one loan and ended up in default. We were further saddled with penalties in addition to seemingly never-ending interest. If payments had been organized, this never would have happened. That's why it is crucial to stay organized and up to date on your student loans, and repair a default situation as quickly as possible.

Use the Personal Student Loan chart that you created in Chapter 1, "Evaluating Your Student Debt Situation," to look at your loan statuses. When you look at your chart, pay attention to any loans that are in default status *and* the ones you forgot about that could go into default status. After all, if you can catch them before the default is official, you can contact your servicer and start making payments before you have to go through default rehab.

How Defaults Affect You

Whether you are currently in default or on the brink, you need to know what the penalties are. This way you can contact your servicer to set up payments if you haven't fallen off the cliff yet. If you have, you'll need to contact your guaranty agency so you can bounce back from your default.

Based on information from www.studentaid.ed.gov, possible penalties for defaulting on a student loan include the following:

- Your college transcripts could be held.
- Student loan repayment program options become more limited.
- You may become ineligible for additional federal student aid.
- Your account may be turned over to a collection agency and you'll have to pay additional charges, late fees, and collection costs, all of which become part of your debt.
- The default could show on your credit reports—and affect your credit scores—for years into the future.
- The drop in credit scores could cause you problems qualifying for credit cards, a car loan, a mortgage, or renting an apartment.
- Federal and state income tax refunds could be withheld and applied to student loan debt on defaulted loans.
- Portions of your wages could be garnished.

- Employers who check credit may reject you as a job candidate.
- You could get turned down for a government job.

But what can you do you about it? Find out the status of your defaulted loans. According to Martha Holler from Sallie Mae, which services both private and federal loans, there are two initial steps you should take if you are delinquent and nearing default:

1. It takes 270 days of making no payments to default on your federal student loans. However, you could have a loan listed as seriously delinquent because you have missed a few payments but haven't missed enough to reach default yet. If this is the case, talk with your servicer and arrange to start making payments again immediately. Whew! Crisis averted.

2. After 270 days of nonpayment, federal regulation says that your lender may consider your loan in default. At this point, your loan is transferred to a guaranty agency that works on behalf of the U.S. Department of Education to collect your loan. If you are past the 270-day mark but still in the first 60 days of the default collection stage, you can avoid the collection fee if you contact your guaranty agency and pay the balance in full.

But what if you don't have a few thousand dollars lying around to pay off your defaulted loan immediately? Don't despair. There are ways to rehabilitate your default.

STEPS FOR DEFAULT RECOVERY

Once you know that you have a defaulted loan, you need to immediately call your guaranty agency and make payment arrangements. Depending on the amount of the loan, you probably won't be able to pay off the whole amount right away. Thus, you will most likely have to set up a payment plan.

Follow these steps for getting your loan out of default and making a payment plan:

1. Call your guaranty agency and ask for a payment plan.

2. Provide as much information as possible to the customer service agent about your financial circumstances so you can set up a payment plan you can reasonably afford. Beginning July 2014, all agencies will be required to offer an income-based default rehabilitation. In the meantime, guaranty agencies have the option of

deciding what is affordable based on your individual circumstances. If you're not offered a payment that is reasonable to you, call a second agent or ask for a supervisor. Whenever anything is decided subjectively, you always want to ask two different customer service agents.

3. Ask about time periods for rehabilitating your loan for getting new loans, consolidation, and removal of the default note from your credit report.

4. Choose a way to pay to ensure that payments are made each month, either through direct debit or automatic payments through your checking or savings account.

5. Confirm with your guaranty agency when your payments are done that a request has been made to all three credit bureaus (Equifax, TransUnion, and Experian) to remove the default from your records. The late payments will still appear, but at least it won't look like you don't make your loan payments.

6. Verify that the default on your credit report is removed by ordering credit reports from all three bureaus for free on www.annual creditreport.com.

While it may be tempting to consolidate your loans ASAP, remove all fingers from your pen or Enter button until you've read the next paragraph.

According to Martha Holler from Sallie Mae, consolidating your federal loans after three on-time payments helps you avoid most repercussions such as wage garnishment and an inability to get new student loans if you return to school. But your loan will still be

> ### Caution
>
> You won't get rid of your federal student loan default on your credit report unless you complete the full default rehabilitation process. Otherwise, your default typically stays on your credit report for seven years.

listed on your credit report as defaulted for seven years! Making just six more on-time monthly payments makes your federal loan eligible for "rehabilitation." At this point, your loan will be reissued by the Department of Education. Or, if it is an FFELP loan, it is eligible to be sold by your guarantor to a new lender, and you can establish a new payment term.

Once your rehabilitated loan is purchased by a new lender, the guarantor instructs the national credit bureaus and your original lender to remove the derogatory credit marks previously reported and you can start with a relatively clean slate. Although you may still see missed payments on your credit report, your report won't be tainted by the student loan equivalent of a car repossession or a foreclosed home.

And remember that those payments, nine months in total, are set as "reasonable and affordable" based on your financial situation.

Exciting update! In July 2014, default rehab is getting an overhaul. While currently what is considered a reasonable and affordable payment during default is up to the discretion of the student loan servicer, the standard will be uniform across all servicers! Income-based repayment will now be part of the equation, so you could theoretically have a payment of $5 and still get out of default. Also, wage garnishment could end after the fifth payment, says Jacqueline Fairbarin, Vice President, Policy and Regulatory Compliance, Great Lakes Higher Education Guaranty Corporation. Never give up hope. Most student loan situations are manageable if you have the knowledge needed to make good choices.

Checklist for Recovering from a Loan Default

✓ Go through your Personal Student Loan chart and find the student loans you don't have payments listed for. Call these companies and ask if your loan is in default or when it could go into default.

✓ When you set up a payment arrangement, ask for payments based on your income.

✓ Don't postpone dealing with the issue—remember, your financial circumstances will be hurt worse if your wages end up being garnished.

✓ Keep track of when the default period ends.

✓ Follow up with your guaranty agency to verify that the default is removed from your credit report after nine consecutive, on-time payments.

> **Caution**
>
> Make sure the default wasn't in error. If you see a default on your record that you think you paid or are currently paying, go through old bank statements or call your current or former bank to request the bank statements for the months you made payments. A few moments spent combing through your old bank statements could save you thousands of dollars of paying back money you don't owe.

Affording Your Payments

Throughout this book you'll learn about various student loan repayment options as well as budgeting techniques that will make your student loan payments a lot more livable. But first you need to figure out if you can handle your student loan payments now. Why is this important? Because if you take a few weeks to finish this book—or more—I don't want you to default on one or more of your student loans because of lack of funds in the meantime.

To figure out how you're doing with your student loan payments, take this pop quiz:

1. Are you making your payments on time each month? ___ yes ___ no

2. Are you making payments on all your student loans (look at your Personal Student Loan chart you created in Chapter 1 for reference)? ___ yes ___ no

3. Have you had to incur credit card debt or withdraw money from your savings account just to pay your monthly student loan bills? ___ yes ___ no

4. Have you missed payments in the last six months because you couldn't afford to make your payment? ___ yes ___ no

If you answered no to questions 1 and 2 or yes to questions 3 and 4, you need to figure out how to fix your situation—fast. Was it a temporary situation that you have since recovered from? If so, you have time to review repayment options while you work on tweaking your budget.

If the situation is ongoing, you have two options:

- If you can find a way to make payments for a two- or three-month time period, you can take a week or two to review your budget and look at options such as consolidation that would extend your loan term but reduce your payment quite a bit. (See Chapter 3, "Consolidating Your Federal Loans.")

- If you can't, you need to call your servicer immediately to discuss temporary reprieves from making payments or payment plans based on your income. If you get a temporary reprieve for six months, you'll have time to tweak your budget and review all your payment options.

No matter what option you choose, double-check your Personal Student Loan chart to make sure all loans you still owe money on are factored into the equation. You may think you have plenty of time to review your options because you are able to afford all your payments, only to discover you're making payments on just four out of five loans.

Checklist for Affording Your Payments

✓ Determine whether you are managing to make all your student loan payments each month without charging on credit cards or dipping into your savings account.

✓ If you are managing your payments well, you have time to review your budget and compare repayment options.

✓ If you can't afford your payments, take action immediately before a loan defaults. Talk to your servicer to discuss your options today.

Deferments and Forbearance

The scariest thing about having any recurring bill is the thought of one day losing your job or getting a reduction in pay where you can no longer afford your payments. This is one area where student loans are better than credit card debt, car loans, and mortgages, because there is a built-in program for missing payments when you are laid off or face other economic emergencies: forbearance and deferments. Using a deferment or forbearance will allow you time to get your situation straightened out by giving you a temporary reprieve from making student loan payments.

Deferments are always preferred because in a deferment situation the government pays the interest on your subsidized student loans for you. Since the government has to shell out money to pay your interest, you will normally have to show proof to your lender of your qualifying deferment situation, such as for active duty military.

Most of us used an in-school deferment—an unlimited deferment—while we attended college with at least a part-time status. If we didn't—and we didn't make payments—we probably would have defaulted before graduation.

Economic deferments require proof of your income to show that you meet the current standards for this deferment type. Economic deferments are limited to three years. For a current list of situations and qualifications for deferment, go to http://studentaid.gov.

A forbearance is generally much easier to get than a deferment and falls into two categories: mandatory and discretionary.

A mandatory forbearance is one the servicer has to grant you if you meet qualifications. Mandatory forbearance is typically required for a borrower that serves in a medical or dental internship or residency program, has a total federal student loan payment that is 20% or more than monthly gross income, serves in specific national service positions such AmeriCorp, performs service that would qualify for loan forgiveness under the teacher loan forgiveness program, for military service, or for a borrower that qualifies for partial repayment programs offered by the Department of Defense.

Discretionary forbearance decisions are up to the servicer. A common type of discretionary forbearance is for when you have a short-term financial problem and need a payment break but don't qualify for economic deferment.

There's good news and bad news about discretionary forbearance. You used to have a limit of three years of forbearance time, but now the servicer can approve you for as long as you need.

> ### Caution
> Do not stop making payments until you know you are approved for your deferment or forbearance. Otherwise, you'll get a ding on your credit report.

The best course of action is to explain your financial situation and ask about other options such as income-based repayment or possibly getting on an extended repayment plan.

For example, let's say you're squeaking by on a paycheck-to-paycheck basis. Getting a breather from your student loan payments sure would be helpful right now. So you sign up for forbearance for your full three years. Your income grows and you learn how to budget better. The extra money you're getting is coming in handy for getting a new car, going out with friends, and getting a nicer apartment. But at the end of the three years, the $40,000 in student loans at 6 percent interest you started with has grown to $47,640.

Would you have been better off squeaking by for a few months or a year while you made your student loan payments?

You shouldn't use forbearance too often. However, you can use this time as a temporary reprieve if you need to pay off a credit card or if you had unpaid sick days, and without the reprieve you'd have to miss a mortgage payment to pay your student loan bill. Taking three to six months to get the rest of your financial life in order is not a bad thing. But you must stay focused, or you'll use up your forbearance without anything positive to show for it.

Track when and why you used deferments and forbearance, for how long, and what type of forbearance or deferment you used. For instance, you may use a forbearance for a couple of months to take a break from student loans. A few months later, you use it because you have excess car repair bills.

You may find from this exercise that you used your deferments and forbearance wisely or that you should have saved your deferments and forbearance for a better occasion. The point is not to feel bad about how you used your deferments and forbearance in the past but to change your habits for the future.

Construct a chart, listing all of your current loans for the rows. Use the following categories for columns:

- Deferment or forbearance
- Type of deferment or forbearance
- Months used
- Date used
- Reason used
- Would you still have used this forbearance if you had to remake that decision

If you consolidated, include your consolidated loan but do not list each loan that is part of your consolidated loan.

Checklist for Deferments and Forbearance

✓ Only use forbearance or deferment when you absolutely need it. You don't want to use your forbearance to make your life more comfortable when your budget is tight but livable.

✓ Always ask for a deferment before forbearance because for deferments for subsidized loans, the government pays interest during the deferment time.

✓ Include a page in your student loan file to keep track of the number of months you have used forbearance or deferment.

✓ It's okay to use your forbearance or deferment at least once in your lifetime to get rid of credit card debt that you plan on not rebuilding or to save for buying a home. Just make sure you don't do either for more than six months.

✓ While deferments are available if you return to school to complete your degree or start a new one, don't go to school for the deferment. Make sure there is a career goal that makes sense for your financial future attached to this degree.

✓ Types and qualifications for deferment and forbearance can change. Before choosing an option, always discuss available options with your lender and review current options at www. studentaid.ed.gov.

Implications of Missing a Student Loan Payment

Your monthly expenses are getting the best of you and you decide to skip just one student loan payment. The next month you apply for a car loan and are denied. The reason: The car dealership checked your credit and your credit score dropped from the previous month. Even worse, you decide to apply for a job with the federal government that will pay you enough that you won't have to worry so much every month about money. You aren't hired because you can't be delinquent 30 days on any kind of federal loan to qualify for a government position.

While the penalties for missing even one payment are rather harsh, student loans have the most ways of any loan to postpone payment—if you speak with your servicer first—or to reduce your payment by going on an extended payment plan, graduated plan, or consolidated plan.

Further, if you are under forbearance or deferment and you don't make a payment, your credit is unharmed. This is because contractually you have several options for forbearance or deferment that you can qualify for based on your situation, such as a layoff or returning to school.

If you have missed payments because you've forgotten to send in a check, set up direct debit with your servicer. You will likely get a quarter percent discount on your interest rate as a bonus for signing up for your payments to come out of your bank account each month.

> ### Caution
>
> Don't stop sending in checks until you get confirmation in the mail or online that your direct debit request has been processed and will start with the next payment date. Call a representative to verify this as well. You don't want to end up with late payments on your credit report simply because you were waiting for direct debit to start.

Regardless of whether it's from forgetting to send in a check or not having the cash, you might occasionally miss a payment. But as long you take action beforehand, you can keep this blunder from happening.

Checklist for Missed Payment Implications

✓ Make your student loan payment a priority in your budget.

✓ When you can't pay your loan, use forbearance or deferment.

✓ Call your servicer before you miss a payment.

✓ If you are forgetful, set up direct debit with your servicer so your loan payment is automatically taken out of your account each month.

Loan Forgiveness

The idea of your student loans magically being forgiven may seem like someone should pinch you because you must be dreaming. You will never have your student loan debt disappear before your very eyes, but there are ways of getting your student loans forgiven.

In this section, you'll learn about public service loan forgiveness, a nifty program for those who work for the government or a nonprofit business [501(c3)] while making ten years of student loan payments. You'll also learn about some of the other student loan forgiveness programs out there and whether it's worth it for you to fulfill the qualifications required.

PUBLIC SERVICE LOAN FORGIVENESS

You've probably heard about the new program offered by the federal government to forgive loans for public service employees after ten years of public service. But maybe you're not sure whether you'll still be in your current job position six months from now, let alone ten years down the road. Should you sign up if you don't know what your ten-year plan is? Which loans qualify, and are there any special rules you should know about?

Work for the government as long as you wish, but don't stay in a job if you no longer enjoy it, especially if you find a better-paying job in the private sector. Follow all the rules to qualify, just in case you do stay on in a government or 501(c3) position for ten years.

Fill out and submit the Employment Certification form to the Department of Education as soon possible to verify that you qualify. You can find the link on the resources page on graduationdebt.org.

Also, carefully pick repayment plans if you think you will need public service loan forgiveness. You have to be on the standard ten-year repayment plan or one of the income-based options: income-based, income-contingent, or Pay as You Earn. If you choose a standard ten-year repayment, you probably won't see much benefit from getting the remainder of your loans forgiven after ten years. Choose one of the income-based options if you qualify.

Debunking Common Myths About Public Service Loan Forgiveness

A member of the Department of Education debunks the common myths and helps you get to the facts behind the Public Service Loan Forgiveness Program.

Myth: You have to sign up for the Public Service Loan Forgiveness Program to earn forgiveness on the remainder of your student loans after ten years.

Fact: You do not have to fill out any paperwork until your ten years of loan repayment and qualifying work have been completed.

Myth: You have to work for the government to qualify for the Public Service Loan Forgiveness Program.

Fact: You can qualify for the Public Service Loan Forgiveness Program by working for any level of government from city government to federal government as well as for any 501(c) qualified not-for-profit organization. When in doubt as to whether your job qualifies, call the Department of Education.

Myth: Payments made within the Direct Loan Program on October 1, 2007, count toward public service loan forgiveness.

Fact: Any payments made on October 2, 2007, or later count toward the 120 payments required to earn public service loan forgiveness.

Myth: If you return to school, your public service time starts over.

Fact: If you return to school, your payment clock is put on hold until you are no longer in in-school deferment status. However, any qualifying employment during that period will not count. Only employment while you are making payments on your student loans counts. New loans you acquire while in school may be covered by the Public Service Loan Forgiveness Program, as long as the law doesn't change before you graduate. However, the repayment and employment clocks on these loans begin after you leave school and enter repayment on the new loans.

For instance, let's say you've built up two years of on-time loan repayments and public service employment before returning to school for an MBA in August 2010. Two years later when you graduate in August 2012, you've borrowed another $40,000. You can be forgiven for your original loans in 2020, after another eight years of repayment on the first loans and eight more years of qualifying employment. Forgiveness on any balances from your new loans would not be available until 2022, assuming you had made 120 payments and been employed in one or more qualifying agencies all that time.

Myth: You can be partially forgiven under the Public Service Loan Forgiveness Program.

Fact: Public service loan forgiveness is an all-or-nothing program. You must have made all of the required 120 on-time monthly payments and been employed in a qualifying public service job during that entire period for the remainder of your loans to be forgiven. Partial loan forgiveness is not awarded if, say, you complete seven or eight years of public service work.

Myth: Approved temporary reprieves count toward the 120 payments required for public service loan forgiveness.

Fact: You have to make 120 payments, so your payment clock stops during periods of deferment or forbearance and resumes after your forbearance or deferment ends.

Myth: In order to earn public service loan forgiveness, you have to work for the same place for ten years.

Fact: The Public Service Loan Forgiveness Program is extremely flexible in that you just have to have been employed during all of the time when you were making the required 120 monthly payments. For instance, you could take a year or two off to work at another job outside of a public service position, you could have a short-term disability, or you could take time off to start a family. The important thing is that your loans won't be forgiven until you have ten years of public service under your belt and at least 120 months of payments while you accumulate your public service time.

ADDITIONAL LOAN FORGIVENESS PROGRAMS

Public service loan forgiveness is only the tip of the loan forgiveness iceberg. There are numerous other programs that may give you money to pay off your student loans. Unfortunately, though, some of these programs could melt before you get a chance to use them, such as state programs that depend on the money being available in your state's budget. Other programs, though not necessarily loan forgiveness programs, are better bets because you can get the money up front, such as companies you work for that will pay for your tuition ahead of time or offer semester-by-semester reimbursement when you return to school, making it easy to take out a loan and be reimbursed within a few months.

Demystifying Loan Forgiveness Programs

Thomas L. Harnisch of the American Association of State Colleges and Universities lets you know what you should be aware of if you have or wish to utilize a loan forgiveness or tuition reimbursement program.

Myth: Loan forgiveness programs apply to all types of student loans.

Fact: It depends on the program. For instance, some federal programs may forgive Perkins Loans, but not Stafford Loans. Private student loans are often excluded from these programs. Choose a loan forgiveness program based on inclusion of the type of loans that you have.

Myth: You have to work for the government to qualify for a loan forgiveness program.

Fact: Some corporations and nonprofits may pay for coursework relevant to an industry, such as an MBA program. Check with your supervisor and human resources department for program requirements. You may have a tuition reimbursement program for returning to school or a loan forgiveness program where you work right now.

Myth: The new programs are the most lucrative for paying off loans.

Fact: The U.S. military's loan forgiveness program has been around for decades and will currently pay back up to $65,000 worth of federal student loans.

Myth: You have to be right out of school to enroll in a loan forgiveness program.

Fact: Not always. It depends on the program requirements. You can often enroll in a loan forgiveness program if you have been out of school for a number of years.

Myth: State-funded loan forgiveness programs are reliable and can assist with your loans when you graduate.

Fact: State-funded loan forgiveness plans are at the mercy of over-stressed state budgets. Some states have reduced funding to these programs, while other states have discontinued programs entirely.

Myth: Once you are enrolled in a program, the amount of your loan forgiven will not change from year to year.

Fact: Especially on the state level, as budget demands change, the amount you are given for loan forgiveness can change.

Myth: You can't confirm you'll receive the money on any state loan forgiveness programs.

Fact: There are both in-school and out-of-school programs. In-school programs will pay for your schooling "up front" in exchange for a work commitment after you graduate. On-the-job loan forgiveness does not pay for schooling, but allows you to "work off" the student loans.

Myth: If a federal or state agency offers loan forgiveness programs, you will automatically qualify if you get the job.

Fact: Not always. Check with the human resources department in each agency, as these programs have different requirements for each agency and job position. Some federal or state agencies may offer generous forgiveness programs, while others may not offer any programs.

Bottom line: As long as you know the restrictions and play by the rules, loan forgiveness programs can help your financial bottom line. Just make sure you are entering a career you love. Otherwise, the partial or total forgiveness of your loans may not be worth what you could be making, in a job that you might enjoy more.

Checklist for Loan Forgiveness Programs

✓ Fill out and submit the Employment Certification form as soon as possible to determine if you qualify for public service loan forgiveness.

✓ To get the full benefit of the Public Service Loan Forgiveness Program, choose an income-based, income-contingent, or Pay as You Earn repayment plan for paying back your loans. If you pay off your loan in ten years, you'll have nothing left to be forgiven.

✓ Don't choose a profession based solely on loan forgiveness or tuition reimbursement. You want to choose a job you'll be happy with, whether or not your loans will be forgiven.

✓ Find out from your employer what programs are available for loan forgiveness and tuition reimbursement. You may get a pleasant surprise and find out you can benefit from these programs where you are employed.

Adjusting Withholding

How many times have you heard in your lifetime that getting a tax refund at the end of the year means you've been giving the IRS an interest-free loan all year long? If you're like me, probably every other day. So how can you avoid getting a tax refund, pay less in taxes all year long, and use the money to pay down your student loans? Use the IRS's online Withholding Calculator to calculate your correct allowances on your W-4 form. Go to www.irs.gov.

An *allowance* is an exemption from the IRS that adjusts the amount you pay in taxes. By increasing your allowances on your W-4 form, you'll get less money taken out of your paychecks instead of getting a larger refund at the end of the year. Taking home more money in each paycheck will help you pay your student loans.

Common exemptions are claiming yourself, a dependent (your child), or a spouse. However, you can also adjust your withholding and the number of allowances taken on your W-4 form by using the IRS Withholding Calculator.

> **Caution**
>
> Claiming too many withholding allowances could lead to an unexpected tax payment at the end of the year. Consider if you have a second job or if your employer tends to take out too much or too little in taxes.

The IRS's Withholding Calculator bases your allowances on the exemptions mentioned above, plus other factors such as the deduction for student loan interest.

If you're self-employed, you can adjust the estimated tax payments that you send in each quarter. But be careful. According to IRS representative Jim Southwell, it's common for self-employed individuals to not send in enough taxes throughout the year. (For more from Jim Southwell, check out his interview in Chapter 11, "Paying Off Your Student Loans Early," for a discussion on getting the most out of your student loan interest tax deduction.)

Debunking Tax Filing Myths

Bob Meighan of TurboTax (www.turbotax.com) sets the record straight on getting the most out of your tax refund and adjusting your withholding.

Myth: You should always adjust your withholding if you know you are getting a refund.

Fact: Some people like to get a big refund on April 15. This is their one big financial bonanza of the year. A lot of people choose to save their refund, though. If that's for savings and it's working for them, it's fine with me. However, if you are having trouble making your student loan payments, you should adjust your withholding allowance so that you have additional funds all year long. You can calculate how many withholding allowances you should declare on the IRS's Withholding Calculator at www.irs.gov.

Myth: If you are self-employed, you can't adjust your withholding allowances based on the IRS's Withholding Calculator.

Fact: The Withholding Calculator doesn't take into account the Social Security and Medicare tax payment independent workers include in their quarterly payments to the IRS. But you can calculate approximately how much to send in each quarter by filling out a tax form using TurboTax for the upcoming year based on how much you expect to make. Be careful to not underestimate your taxes and end up owing money at the end of the year. Estimate your taxes slightly on the high side. This way the worst that can happen is to receive a tax refund at the end of the year.

Myth: You are just as likely to get the same refund if you file your return without using tax software.

Fact: Tax software returns that are electronically filed are 20 times more accurate than manually prepared tax returns. Tax software, like TurboTax, not only helps you fill out all the right forms, but asks you questions based on your situation so you get all the tax write-offs to which you're entitled. It also does all the math for you.

Myth: You can't take the tax deduction for interest on your student loans if your parents made the payments.

Fact: Even if your parents paid the interest on your behalf, you can still take the deduction. As long you are legally responsible, you can claim the deduction. For instance, if you have a Stafford Loan, you can and should take the deduction. Your parents can take the deduction on Parent Plus Loans—even if you make the payments.

Myth: If you don't itemize your deductions, you won't qualify for deductions such as the student loan interest tax deduction.

Fact: You may qualify for the student loan interest tax deduction without itemizing. All credits, such as the credits available for college tuition payments, do not require itemizing deductions. However, you may do better if you have a lot of itemized deductions such as mortgage interest, moving expenses, 401k contributions, or charitable giving. Tax programs like TurboTax will tell you whether you have enough of these deductions to itemize.

Myth: If you didn't declare all your deductions in previous years, it's not worth the trouble of filing an amended tax return.

Fact: You can file amended returns for the three prior tax years. If you didn't declare your student loan interest deduction or the tuition credit you were eligible to claim in a prior year, you could be throwing away hundreds of dollars if you don't amend your tax return. You can use past editions of TurboTax to file amended returns to claim student loan, education, and other deductions and credits you didn't know you were eligible to take up to three years ago.

Myth: If you don't think you owe taxes, you shouldn't file a return.

Fact: If you earned income, you should file a return. You may owe taxes after all, or you may be entitled to a refund due to a deduction or credit you weren't thinking about. There are also some credits available for those who have limited income and no income tax.

Myth: Tax software is expensive.

Fact: TurboTax online starts with a free version and goes up from there, depending on your needs.

Bottom line: Don't just fill out the EZ form this year—do some research on the IRS Web site and/or using tax software to find and declare all your deductions and credits.

Checklist for Adjusting Withholding

- ✓ Change your allowances if you received a tax refund this year or are going to have a dramatic change before next year's tax return, such as starting to make payments on your student loans, buying a home, getting married, or having a child.

- ✓ Go to www.irs.gov and use the Withholding Calculator to calculate your allowances.

- ✓ File a new W-4 with your place of employment if you need to adjust your allowances.

- ✓ If you are self-employed, be careful about adjusting your withholding. Your income may change each year, and it's always better to overestimate by a little and get a refund than underestimate by a lot and get a penalty.

Income-Based Repayment Plans

When you have more student loans than your income can handle, your solution may be income-based payments. In an income-based repayment plan, loan payments are based on an annual formula of what individuals can afford based on their income and family size.

Your monthly payment can never be more than what you would pay on a standard ten-year repayment plan, but it can be more than what you would pay on an extended plan. However, if your income is low enough, you may have a monthly payment of zero, but your interest, especially on your unsubsidized loans, will still accrue. For the first three years of income-based repayment, the government will pick up the tab on your interest on your subsidized loans. You have to re-qualify for income-based repayments each year based on your income.

Income-based repayment works best in the following cases:

- You are planning on being on income-based repayment for a year or two to maintain a payment schedule until your income rises.

- You have mostly subsidized loans and your income allows you to pay payments that wouldn't fully cover the interest. You can pay what you can afford to keep your balance from building.

Pay as You Earn: Income-Based Repayment 2.0

Depending on when your loans were issued, as well as if you're currently repaying your loans, you could qualify for the new and improved income-based repayment program titled Pay as You Earn.

WHAT'S SO GREAT ABOUT PAY AS YOU EARN?

With Pay as You Earn, there is potential for lower payments now as well as more that could be forgiven later. The formula for the exact amount of income-based repayments is always based on a percentage of discretionary income—the amount you are above the poverty line based on

---

Caution

Since income-based and Pay as You Earn repayments can be below what your interest is, as far as long-term payoff strategies, you may be better off with a consolidated plan that would reduce and extend your payments while paying off the accrued interest each month.

This is because income-based or Pay as You Earn repayments can be less than the amount of interest you owe that month. Since your interest still accrues—with the exception of the government paying the interest on your subsidized loans for the first three years of income-based repayment—you could end up with your balance being higher than when you entered income-based repayment. However, if your income stays low enough to continue to qualify for income-based payments for a number of years, you could get part of your loan forgiven after 25 years with traditional income-based repayment or after 20 years under the Pay as You Earn program.

family size. The old standard for income-based repayment was 15 percent. With Pay as You Earn, it's only 10 percent.

How much of a difference could this make to your monthly payment? For some, over $100 per month.

But you don't have to figure out what your discretionary income actually is. My best friends are online calculators, and there are links to both traditional income-based and Pay as You Earn calculators on the graduationdebt.org Web site. You just plug in your income and family size and voilà! You can find out your potential payment.

For example, I plugged in numbers for a single person with a modified adjusted gross income of $40,000 with $40,000 in federal student loans who doesn't live in Alaska or Hawaii (Alaska and Hawaii residents may have lower payments due to an adjustment for higher costs of living). The income-based monthly payment calculated at $285, while the Pay as You Earn monthly payment was $190. The bonus? The maximum repayment period was 20 years instead of 25 years.

WHO QUALIFIES?

Pay as You Earn has two qualifications: If you borrowed federal student loans prior to October 1, 2007, they had to have been paid off before that date. You also have to have borrowed one or more federal student loans on or after October 1, 2011.

For example, you borrowed federal student loans to pay for an undergraduate degree you earned in 1995. You're returning to school to pursue a master's in 2014. If your loans are paid off, you would qualify for Pay as You Earn repayments. If not, you can't utilize this program.

Note: Parent loans can't be included in either income-based or Pay as You Earn repayment plans.

Debunking Common Myths About Income-Based Repayment

Want to learn more about income-based repayment? Check out the following interview with a Department of Education staff member.

Myth: The income-based repayment program is only available to direct loan borrowers.

Fact: Any borrower who has FFEL or Direct Loans (or both) and who meets the income eligibility requirements of the program qualifies. If you have loans with more than one lender, your lenders can work together to devise income-based payments for each set of loans. However, it's best if you are going to utilize this program to consolidate your loans with one lender to simplify the process.

Myth: Income-based repayment will always save you money.

Fact: It depends on the individual's situation. This is because an income-based payment can be less than the amount of interest you owe that month. Since your interest still accrues—with the exception of the government paying the interest on your subsidized loans for the first three years of income-based repayment—you could end up with your balance being higher than when you entered income-based repayment. However, if your income stays low enough to continue to qualify for income-based payments for a number of years, you could get part of your loan forgiven after 25 years.

Myth: Income-based repayment replaces income-contingent and income-sensitive payment plans.

Fact: Income-based repayment is a better option for most borrowers who qualify; however, the income-contingent repayment plan for Direct Loan borrowers and the income-sensitive repayment plan for FFEL borrowers are still available.

Myth: Income-based payments are based on your current year's income.

Fact: Income-based payments are calculated based on the previous year's adjusted gross income from your tax return. However, if your income has changed since last year, you can submit a form and proof of changed income.

Myth: Income-based payments are calculated based on your total income.

Fact: Income-based payments are based on your IRS adjusted gross income. Thus, if you have untaxable income such as veteran's benefits, it will not count toward your income eligibility.

Myth: Only your personal income counts for qualifying for income-based payments.

Fact: Your spouse's income counts toward your income as well. However, qualifying income limits vary by family size.

Myth: You have to stay on income-based repayment for the full 25 years to have your remaining debt cancelled.

Fact: Income-contingent, income-sensitive, and standard ten-year plan payments also count toward your 25-year term.

Checklist for Income-Based Repayment

✓ Determine if you qualify for Pay as You Earn first.

✓ Use online calculators to review your repayment options.

✓ Don't assume you're automatically better off with income-based or Pay as Your Earn payments long term. If you expect your income to rise dramatically in the future, you could end up paying more in accumulated interest when you are no longer eligible for these options.

Returning to School

You loathe your job, but you loathe your student loan payments even more. If you go back to school for a master's degree or to finish getting the degree you are paying loans on, you accomplish two tasks: postponing paying your loans until you graduate and training to do something you might like better. But if you're 35 now, do you really want to finish paying off a consolidated loan when you're 67 and ready to retire? Before you decide going back to college is the right step for you, ask yourself the following questions:

- Could you switch jobs without another degree? You might be able to apply your existing skills to a different career. It's not uncommon to perform a job that isn't typical of the degree you hold. For example, how many philosophy majors end up being professional philosophers?

- Are there other job openings where you currently are employed? If you feel like you're in a job rut, you might be able to solve your boredom issues right where you are. Your employer could give you new tasks within your current position, or you could look at department transfers within your own company.

- Do you have a clear focus on what you want to do with your degree when you finish? If you are getting another degree to figure out what you want to do next, you might just get deeper into a student loan money pit.

- Have you done a thorough review of incomes for the jobs you expect to garner with the degree you want? Will you make enough to pay off current and future loans in this field right out of school?

- Have you thought about volunteer work? Charities always need help and volunteering is a great way to develop entirely new skill sets.

- Have you considered doing a shadow day? Following someone around for a day to check out what his or her career is like seems like something you would have done years ago when you were just out of high school or college. But it's still one of the research techniques you should employ when considering a new field.

You already know what it's like to have student loan debt. Before you get more, you want to make sure that you're doing it for the right reasons and it will help your financial future.

If you do decide to back to school, utilize some of the same options you used when you first went to school, such as scholarships, co-op programs, and looking at colleges based on tuition as well as program quality.

There are times when going back to school will work out for you financially in the long run. Just do everything you can to make sure returning to school is the best decision for you before making another leap into more debt.

Checklist for Returning to School

- ✓ Evaluate all other options before returning to school for career advancement or improved workplace enjoyment.

- ✓ Meet with your own boss or human resources to see what options you have within your company.

- ✓ Check Web sites and university career centers for a realistic starting salary for the field you are interested in pursuing, in the city in which you'd like to live.

- ✓ Calculate the additional student loan payment amount you will have upon graduation.

- ✓ Consider trying out the job in some way, through volunteering, shadow days, or internships.

Chapter Wrap-Up

- Review your Personal Student Loan chart from Chapter 1 and your bank statements to make sure you are making payments on all your loans.

- Defaults can become a much heavier weight on your shoulders than the loan itself. Work toward rehabbing your defaults right away.

- Don't wait until you finish this book to choose a repayment option if you might miss a payment first. Contact your servicer to get forbearance or deferment while you evaluate different repayment plans and develop better budgeting skills.

- Don't assume you don't qualify for income-based repayment programs until you've used the repayment calculators on the studentaid.ed.gov Web site. Remember to use the Pay as You Earn calculator if you think you might qualify. The calculator includes questions that help you figure out which income-based plan you should consider.

- Explore all student loan repayment options. Even if your loan amount seems insurmountable now, you have more possible payment plans to make your loans affordable within your budget, options for temporary payment reprieves, and ways to recover financially from late or missed payments than nearly any other kind of loan.

- Having part of your loan forgiven is a great thing, but be careful to choose employment based on what you love and not just the free student loan money attached.

- Repayment plans and deferment and forbearance qualifications can change. Always double-check with your servicer and/or read the facts at www.studentaid.ed.gov before choosing a plan or temporary payment reprieve option.

- Adjusting your tax withholding is a great way to get extra money in your paycheck to put toward your student loan payments.

💲 Plan for career changes by dabbling in your new profession through volunteering, jobs within your own company, or shadow days. Then you can make a careful decision about whether returning to school for another degree is worth it.

3

Consolidating Your Federal Loans

You have $60,000 in student debt and the $675 payment for the standard ten-year repayment plan is taking up a large part of your budget. Pretty soon you're going to have to choose between paying rent and making your student loan payments.

You're thinking about consolidating your loans into one loan with an extended payment plan. But as much as you feel weighed down by a student loan payment that is over $600, you don't feel any better about still making payments 30 years from now.

Or . . .

You did consolidate your loans before October 2007, when lenders were offering a virtual goldmine of student loan savings. You managed to snag a 2 percent interest rate reduction after 36 on-time payments. But you're afraid you might lose your benefits if you can't make payments temporarily because of a pay cut.

Or . . .

You're a government employee who consolidated your loans after October 2007, but you want to reconsolidate your loans to direct lending in order to qualify for public service loan forgiveness after ten years.

Or . . .

You are reconsolidating your student loans because you want to include student loans in your loan from when you returned to school for an advanced degree, such as a master's, a law degree, or a Ph.D.

Or. . .

You consolidated in the last couple of years and want to know what to do if your consolidation loan is sold to another bank, or if you lose your job and temporarily can't make payments.

No matter which of these scenarios represents your situation, there is an easy solution to the problem that involves a few simple steps and analysis of your personal financial situation.

What Is Consolidation?

Federal student loan *consolidation* is when, through one of your current servicers or direct lending, you decide to take all of your current loans and combine them into one new loan. The loans can be all from the same lender or through several lenders.

This is often done to eliminate having to schedule payments with several loans from multiple semesters—leaving you with one streamlined payment. Other reasons for consolidation include securing a fixed interest rate, taking advantage of special deals offered by the lender for consolidating, and reconsolidating to include new student loans. In the past, consolidation was more open. Now, new consolidation loans have to be through direct lending.

Should You Consolidate Your Loans?

If you're not sure whether you should consolidate your loans, it's likely because you're not sure which one is harder to handle: a higher payment now versus a longer period of time to pay off your loans and more interest paid to borrow the money. For example, $60,000 in student debt paid off over ten years with an interest rate of 4.125 percent would cost you $13,325 in interest, for a total of $73,325; while $60,000 in student loans paid off in 30 years at the same interest rate would cost you $44,684 in interest, for a total of $104,684. A 30-year loan costs you $31,359 extra in interest. It seems like as long as you can afford your payments that you should stay on a ten-year plan. Yet, for most people it makes sense to consolidate their loans.

Why?

When you consolidate your loans, your payment is lower, but you can pay off your loans early. You could even decide to go ahead and pay it off in ten years. In the meantime you've got a manageable payment, which may be less than half the payment required in a ten-year repayment plan. Plus, if you have any federal student loans with variable interest rates, consolidation is the only way to get a fixed interest rate. So why would you want to stick with a ten-year plan?

If the ten-year standard payment plan helps you to stay disciplined enough to pay off your student loans in ten years, keep with it. Just make sure you can handle your payment. However, take a look at the Personal Student Loan chart you created in Chapter 1, "Evaluating Your Student Debt Situation," from the information you gathered from the National Student Loan Data System. If your chart shows that you have loans with variable interest rates, consolidate your loans so that you have a guaranteed rate.

It may seem like the smaller consolidated payment will keep you in student loan payments for decades longer. But what it really does is give you a payment you can always afford, and you can add extra money to your payments whenever you like.

Checklist for Deciding Whether to Consolidate Your Loans

✓ Review your budget to see if you can handle your ten-year standard payment.

✓ To find out exactly what your consolidated payment would be, use the online calculator found at https://loanconsolidation.ed.gov. Use this calculator even if you are consolidated with your current servicer who is not direct lending. The length of payments and payment amount will be the same on any federal consolidation loan.

✓ Before deciding to maintain a ten-year standard repayment plan, review your Personal Student Loan chart from Chapter 1 to see if you have any variable rate student loans.

✓ Remember, you can consolidate at a later date if you change your mind.

> **Caution**
>
> You won't necessarily have one consolidated loan when you complete your consolidation, but you will have a consolidated payment. Lenders keep unsubsidized and subsidized loans separate because if you return to school at a later date, the government will temporarily take over your interest payments on your subsidized student loans.

The Coveted Fixed Interest Rate

One of the unique benefits of federal loans versus private loans is having a fixed interest rate. From the day your student loan money first hit your account at your university, you knew that the interest rate you started out with would be the interest rate you would be charged until the day you paid off your loan. However, federal loans with guaranteed, fixed interest rates attached for the life of the loan are a relatively new phenomenon. And even if you graduated yesterday, you could still have some loans without fixed interest rates.

Before July 2006, educational loans had variable rates that could change once a year on July 1. Sometimes the rates go up and sometimes the rates go down. The only way to secure a fixed interest rate on the loans you have before this date is to consolidate your loans.

But what would your fixed interest rate be? For that portion of your loans, it would be fixed at the current interest rate. For example, if you still have loans that were disbursed between July 1, 1998 and June 30, 2006, the current rate between July 1, 2009 and July 1, 2010 for consolidating those loans if you are in repayment is 2.48 percent. If you only have loans from this time period, then 2.48 percent would be your interest rate under consolidation. However, if you have other loans, the interest rate on your consolidation loan would be based on the weighted average of the interest rates.

WEIGHTED INTEREST RATES

Figuring out your weighted interest rate is pretty simple. Each loan is given a weight based on its percentage of the total of all the loans you are consolidating into one. You multiply each one by its assigned interest rate. Then you round it up to the nearest 1/8 percent. Don't worry if you don't know what the nearest 1/8 percent is or don't want to do the calculation. The calculator on the Federal Direct Consolidation Loan Web site will help you calculate everything. You can also find the link in the resources area of my Web site: www.wisebread.com/newgrads.

For an example of the calculation, say you had $50,000 in student loans, and you started college in fall 2004. Your loans are split evenly down the middle between interest rates, with $25,000 of your remaining student debt borrowed before July 1, 2006 and $25,000 of your remaining student loan debt borrowed after July 1, 2006. You graduated in the spring 2008, and consolidated in February 2010. What would your weighted interest rate be?

- For the $25,000 remaining from your loans you borrowed before July 1, 2006, your interest rate is 2.48 percent.

- For the $25,000 you borrowed between July 1, 2006 and July 1, 2008, your interest rate is 6.8 percent. This is because interest rates set for July 1, 2006 to July 1, 2007, and July 1, 2007 to July 1, 2008, were disbursed with fixed interest rates of 6.8 percent.

Your weighted interest rate in consolidation would be:

(50 percent × .0248) + (50 percent × 0.068) = 4.64 percent

Then, you round the interest rate up to the nearest 1/8 percent. Once consolidated, 4.75 percent is the permanent interest rate for the entire loan.

If this loan was consolidated a year earlier with the exact same scenario, the weighted interest rate would have been 5.5 percent. This is because instead of the interest rate being 2.48 percent for the older loans, the interest rate assigned to the variable rate loans was 4.21 percent. For the year before that, the interest rate on the older loans was 7.22 percent. Thus, the consolidated interest rate would have been 7.125 percent (7.01 rounded up to the nearest 1/8 percent).

What does all this mean when it comes to payments? A standard consolidation loan for $50,000 consolidated for 25 years would yield the following payments:

- Consolidated payment at 4.75 percent: $285.06

- Consolidated payment at 5.5 percent: $307.04

- Consolidated payment at 7.125 percent: $357.39

So, if you consolidated between July 1, 2009, and July 1, 2010, you would have saved about $24 per month for 25 years versus the year before—that's the equivalent of approximately six espresso drinks! And the difference between the 4.75 percent and 7.125 percent payments is about $72—that's a whopping 18 espresso drinks!

Variable rates have a maximum of 8.5 percent. Thus, the average with the situation I just discussed would be 7.75 percent (7.65 rounded up to the nearest 1/8 percent). The payment with an interest rate of 7.75 percent is $377.66, which is about $92—or 23 espresso drinks—more than the 4.75 percent loan payment!

Luckily, the consolidated fixed rate for variable rate federal loans has stayed in the 2.3 to 2.5 percent range over the last few years, but interest rates can always rise in a future year. Lesson? Consolidate your variable rate federal student loans while rates are this low.

Should You Wait to Consolidate Based on the Current Interest Rate?

If all your federal student loans have fixed interest rates, then you can consolidate whenever you like. Current rates are never a concern. Just verify this fact by looking at each of your loans on the National Student Loan Data System (www.nslds.ed.gov) or review your Personal Student Loan chart from Chapter 1.

Even if you do have variable rate loans, generally, you still don't want to wait to consolidate. Interest rates can go up and down. The only time it's worthwhile to wait is if you are thinking about consolidating in June and you've heard news that rates are expected to get lower on July 1.

Then you are close enough to the interest rates resetting to follow the 91-day T-bill rate that is the basis for variable student loan rates. You can find these rates on investment Web sites and on the news.

For the exact interest rate terms of your loans, check out the following table.

Variable Rate Terms by Loan Disbursement Date for Federal Loans			
Loan Disbursement Date Range	Loan Status	Interest Rate Calculation	Maximum Interest Rate
7/1/1994 to 6/30/1995	Any	91-day T-bill + 3.1	8.25
7/1/1995 to 6/30/1998	Repayment or forbearance	91-day T-bill + 3.1	8.25
7/1/1998 to 6/30/2006	Repayment or forbearance	91-day T-bill + 2.3	8.25

The bottom line is that any fixed rate you receive is better than any variable rate. With a fixed rate, you can plan your budget better when you know your payment won't change each year.

INTEREST RATES DURING YOUR GRACE PERIOD

No matter when you consolidate, you can get an interest rate break on your variable rate loans for consolidating during your grace period (the six months after graduation), while you are still in school or during a period of approved deferment. The interest rate break is normally about 0.5 percent.

Checklist for Fixing Your Interest Rate

✓ Check the National Student Loan Data System Web site (www.nslds.ed.gov) or your Personal Student Loan chart

Caution

You don't have to choose a consolidated plan to get extended repayments. Why wouldn't you want one easy payment? Let's say you have fixed-rate federal student loans with two different lenders. Some loans were borrowed in years when interest rates were higher than others. You may want to keep your loans separate so when you send in extra cash when you can, you can choose for the payment to go toward the highest interest loan.

from Chapter 1 for whether you have any variable interest rate loans.

✓ If you have variable rate loans, check the Department of Education's Web site (http://loanconsolidation.ed.gov) for your current interest rate. This will be the rate for the variable rate portion of your student loans.

✓ Calculate the weighted average of your student loans by first multiplying the percentage each loan is of your total loans by its corresponding interest rate. Then add up all the results to find what your interest rate would be on a consolidated loan.

✓ If you have variable rate loans, consolidate them so you can begin to budget for your loans based on a payment that will be the same until your loan is completely paid off.

More Benefits to Consolidating

While securing a fixed interest rate on your variable rate loans is an enormous benefit of loan consolidation, it's just one of several benefits to consolidation.

ONE CONSOLIDATED PAYMENT

The biggest benefit to consolidation has always been having only one payment to make each month. If you still owe the same amount of money, why is this a benefit? Because your credit score is partially based on how well you maintain your accounts. Therefore, if you only have one payment, you are less likely to forget to make a payment and ding your credit score.

Also, when you have eight different loans, one loan can slip through the cracks and you may forget about it. I know I did. I had all my other loans in forbearance, except for one loan that I forgot about, and it went into default. I had to wait until I made enough payments on my defaulted loan for it to be accepted for consolidation. But once I consolidated after making a few on-time payments, I never forgot another loan payment. It's been five years. I have one loan payment that automatically comes out of my account through direct debit.

AFFORDABLE EXTENDED PAYMENTS

When you have at least $40,000 in student loan debt, it's helpful to have lower payments. You may not need the full 25 years to pay off your loan, but there are times where the lower payment can come in handy:

- **When you want to buy a house.** Banks look at your total monthly debt payments as well as your credit scores to see if you are a good lending risk. And lower payments means you are likely to afford your mortgage payment.

- **When you have a major life change.** Losing your job, having a baby, planning your wedding, or facing a health crisis are just some of the major life changes that can impact your financial situation.

You can always put extra money toward your monthly payments, but you will have the security of knowing you can make your payments now. For the exact time frame of your consolidation loan, check out the following table.

Amount Owed	Years to Pay	Number of Payments
$10,000 to $19,999	15	180
$20,000 to $39,999	20	240
$40,000 to $59,999	25	300
$60,000 and up	30	360

How to Consolidate Your Loans

You're ready to consolidate your loans, now you just have to complete the process using the following steps:

1. **Gather information on your loans.** Grab the Personal Student Loan chart you completed in Chapter 1. You will need to have the following information on your open loans: the servicer, the interest rate, and the loan status. Whether you consolidate with direct lending or one of your current lenders, you'll be asked for this information online or over the phone for the following reasons:

   - **Servicer:** The consolidator has to know who to contact to pay off the old lender in order to transfer the loan.

   - **Interest rate:** So your new interest rate can be calculated, your new lender needs to know what all your old interest rates were. Your consolidated loan interest rate is the weighted average of your current loans.

- **Loan status:** You can't consolidate a defaulted loan until you've made payment arrangements with your guaranty agency and followed the payment plan for at least three months. Unsubsidized versus subsidized is also important for the loan status. If you have both kinds of loans, you will have one consolidated subsidized loan and one consolidated unsubsidized loan. Finally, if your loans have already been consolidated, you can reconsolidate only in two circumstances: if you have unconsolidated loans to add into your consolidated loan, or if you are reconsolidating into direct lending.

2. **Fill out the forms.** With direct lending, you can fill in all your loan information online and e-sign the form. You can also print the forms and mail them in. If you are consolidating with another lender with whom you currently have federal loans, you should contact them to ask whether applications are accepted online, by mail, or by giving information to a representative over the phone. Even if you are diligent, you still want to watch to make sure the first payments post, especially if you filled out a direct debit form.

3. **Don't stop making payments on your old loans until you know your consolidation is complete.** This is the easiest way that good intentions can go horribly wrong. You consolidate your loans to make sure you never miss a payment, then you do miss a payment while waiting for your loan to be consolidated. Wait until you have some sort of written confirmation of your consolidation's completion and the date of your first payment before you stop making payments on your previous loans.

4. **Follow up, follow up, and follow up some more.** Keep track of your loan consolidation process by checking either online or making a phone call every two or three weeks. If you forgot to sign mailed-in forms or if there's some other holdup, you want to know right away what it is so you can fix it.

Checklist for Consolidating Your Loans

✓ Gather all the information on your student loans and have it with you when you are filling out forms.

✓ Check with your servicer to see how they prefer to receive the forms, then e-mail or mail them.

✓ Don't stop making payments on your loans until you've received written confirmation that your consolidation is complete.

✓ Follow up on your consolidation to stay on top of any problems.

Benefits Before October 2007

You may have been lucky enough to have gotten one of the fantastic student loan deals available before October 2007. Or you may have heard from friends about incredible deals they received when consolidating their federal student loans: 2 percent interest rate deduction after 36 months of on-time payments, 1 percent interest rate deduction after 24 months, or a 3 percent cash rebate after 6 months of on-time payments. So what's your first thought when you also have large amounts of student loan debt? Sign me up for the free money or interest rate discounts!

Unfortunately, "sign me up" is no longer an option. In October 2007, the government cut off subsidies to private lenders participating in loan consolidation. Thus, huge interest rate discounts and rebates were no longer profitable for your lenders. However, if you have these benefits, you need to know how to hang onto them.

I work really hard to earn my benefits. When I consolidated, I found a consolidation deal that gave me 2 percent off my loan after 36 on-time payments. If I complete all my on-time payments, I'll shave eight years off my loan. How? While my payments remain the same, the amount of my payment going toward interest goes down after month 36 of my loan.

The following table shows how a loan very similar to mine, with around $60,000 left, would change if the interest rate went down 2 percent after the first three years. It assumes an interest rate of 4.5 percent with a monthly payment of $304.01.

$60,000 Federal Loan Consolidated for 30 Years				
Month	Interest Paid per Month	Principal Paid per Month	Interest Paid per Month if Loan Adjusts to 2.5% After 36 On-Time Payments	Principal Paid per Month
1	$225.00	$79.01	$225.00	$79.01
37	$213.60	$90.41	$118.67	$185.34
120 (10 years)	$180.66	$123.35	$83.72	$220.29
240	$110.73	$193.28	$21.23	$282.78
273	$85.32	$218.69	$1.12	$302.89
360	$1.13	$302.88	Paid off over 7 years earlier	

The balance left on a loan at 4.5 percent at the same time the adjusted interest rate loan reaches 0 is over $22,000.

How Can You Lose Your Benefits?

A missed payment can be a total accident or it can happen because you didn't have the money. Common reasons for a missed payment include failing to put in a new direct debit form and not making a manual payment in the meantime, or being late on a payment because you forgot the due date. All of these are completely avoidable. If you are unable to make a payment for financial reasons, you can contact your servicer to arrange for a temporary payment reprieve (see Chapter 2, "Organizing Your Student Debt Payments"). You can make manual payments until your direct debit form is processed. You can set up direct debit or bill pay to make sure you payments always arrive on time.

If you pay ahead to make sure you don't miss a payment, you could inadvertently miss a payment. This is because if your payment is not made within the payment grace period—even if you're early—it doesn't count for that month. For example, if your due date is on the 15th of the month, your terms may say that you have to make your payment within ten days of the 15th. The safest way to avoid losing benefits for this reason is to make your payment on the exact due date. If you're mailing in the payment, mail it at least one week before the due date to ensure that it gets there on time.

Once you've completed the payments required to earn the benefit you were offered, your benefit is secured and can't be taken away.

How to Dispute Loss of Consolidation Benefits

You consolidated at the right time to get consolidation benefits with a reduction in your interest rate of 2 percent after 36 on-time payments. The problem is you forgot to send in one of your payments, or a payment wasn't made during a transition period from direct debit from your old bank account to your new one. You just received a letter saying that your benefits are no longer valid. What do you do?

Unfortunately, if you were lucky enough to consolidate with special benefits, you also had the possibility of losing those benefits at some point due to a missed payment. But if you are proactive now, you may be able to get your benefits reinstated. If this is your first time missing a payment, emphasize this with the phone representative for your servicer. You can also make points by pointing out the following:

- A record of on-time payments
- If the letter received was in error because you have an approved forbearance or deferment
- If you returned to school and have at least half-time status
- If you didn't make a payment while waiting for a debit form to be processed

The longer you wait to contact your servicer, the harder it will be to argue your point. The servicer wants to know if this is a one-time discrepancy.

Checklist for Maintaining Consolidation Benefits

✓ Make all payments on time.

✓ Call your servicer when you can't afford your payments to get a temporary payment reprieve.

✓ Let your servicer know when you are returning to school and file the appropriate paperwork.

✓ Be proactive and contact your servicer if you miss a payment to reduce the chance of permanently losing your benefits.

✓ Don't start making extra payments on this type of loan until you've earned your benefits. Your payments to earn your benefit are counted by a computer, and thus could get confused by payments not made within the grace period or extra amounts added to your regular payments.

✓ Once your benefits are earned and irrevocable, that is the time to make extra payments on your loans.

Deferment and Forbearance Options with Consolidation

You just lost your job and you're calculating the previous forbearance time you've used on your loans. But wait—you consolidated. All forbearance and deferment time limits have been reset. You now have three years of general forbearance time available in 12-month increments on your consolidation loan.

It's relatively easy to get forbearance on a consolidated loan—you don't have to call multiple servicers to get forbearance on each individual loan. This saves you from possibly forgetting one loan and getting a ding on your credit report, or worse, having your loan default three to six months later. But in the spirit of maintaining your credit scores, you still have to call your servicer to request forbearance and wait to stop making payments until your forbearance has been approved.

As I discussed in Chapter 2, you'll want to save forbearance for when you really need it. Once you've consolidated, unless you reconsolidate with direct lending from another lender, request a new consolidation because of additional loans or you won't get any more forbearance time added to your account.

Deferments have tougher rules for acceptance, but you can still get one if you return to school or are active duty in the military and called away to serve your country. You also get a brand-new, three-year term for economic deferment. If you are working full-time and making less than 150 percent of the poverty line in your state, can't afford your payments, or are in the Peace Corps, you can request an economic deferment instead of forbearance. This way, if you have subsidized loans, the government will pay the interest on the loan during your deferment period. (See Chapter 2 for more information.)

Whether you utilize a deferment or forbearance, remember that your loan amount will not decrease. In fact, you could end up owing thousands more after a couple of years of forbearance because of accrued interest. In order to negate this effect, try making small payments until you get back on your feet.

Checklist for Using Forbearance and Deferments When Your Loan Is Consolidated

- ✓ Only use forbearance when you absolutely need the temporary reprieve from payments.

- ✓ Don't count previous time left of your three years in your forbearance time. You have a brand-new three years of forbearance time once you consolidate.

- ✓ Remember that you generally will not get new forbearance consolidation time unless you reconsolidate your loans to direct lending from another lender, or you reconsolidate due to new loans.

- ✓ Make small payments on your loans during your reprieve to avoid your loan amount growing from accrued interest.

What if Your Loan Is Sold to Another Bank?

Just like with a car loan or mortgage, your loan can be sold to another lender. However, your contract will carry over, stating how many payments you have left and the borrower benefits. But just because your terms stay the same doesn't mean you don't have to watch the process carefully. Your payments could get lost in the servicer shuffle, direct debit agreements will have to be redone, and payment counts toward a discount could be reported in error if you got special benefits on a loan prior to October 2007.

Although your lenders loaned you the money, you will always call the servicer for customer service on your loans. For example, if your current lender sells your loan to another bank, you would call the number your current lender gives you for the servicer. Then you would contact the servicer of your new lender after the transfer.

DIRECT DEBIT

Fill out new direct debit forms immediately. Pay your loans manually until you get confirmation that your direct debit has started. Just like when you first set up direct debit with your original loan, the process could take a few months. Make manual payments until you get it in writing—either online or by a letter in the mail—that you are on direct debit. Even once you get written confirmation, double-check in your bank account that the money is withdrawn within a week of payment. If not, call your servicer and make a manual payment if necessary. A manual payment means you are writing a check to your servicer instead of having the amount automatically withdrawn from your account. You may also be able to make a payment to your new lender over the phone using a credit card.

This is where direct lending loans have a huge benefit, because more than likely the government will never sell your federal loan to another lender. The loan is backed with government funds and lent directly from those funds.

KEEP TRACK OF ALL PAPERWORK

It's important during the transition period that you make sure you keep track of all your terms just in case your new lender doesn't recognize borrower benefits you received or how many payments you've made.

If you don't have your paperwork handy, no worries. There are a couple of ways you can recover both your payment history and your loan terms:

- Start by calling both the original servicer and the new servicer to ask for the paperwork and payment history on your loan. You want to call both servicers, because in a transition, you won't generally know which one currently holds your loan records until you call.

- Contact your bank for copies of your past bank account statements. Your bank should keep records of your transactions for at least the last seven years.

- If you still have access to your account via the Web site of your past servicer, print the page that shows you are up to date and how many payments you have made.

Checklist for On-Time Payment (Whether or Not You Have a New Lender)

✓ Verify your grace period for rules about early and late payments. You don't want to end up missing a payment because you paid 16 days early and the payment went toward your principal, instead of counting toward your monthly payment.

✓ Check monthly to make sure your payment has posted directly with your servicer.

✓ Keep track of how many payments you have left to secure your borrower benefits.

✓ Schedule either a bill pay through your bank or set up direct debit with your servicer. Direct debit is more effective because your servicer has the information.

✓ Always make manual payments if you change bank accounts or you set up a new direct debit form until you see the first direct debit payment post.

✓ Don't close your old bank account with direct debit until your first student loan payment posts on your new account.

✓ Fill out new direct debit forms immediately with your servicer.

Stray Loans After Consolidation

All your loans are finally consolidated. Big sigh of relief—only one loan payment to make. Time to pop the cork! But hold on to that little piece of wood because you may need to put it back in the bottle for another 60 days. Why? One or more student loans were lost in the shuffle and left out of the consolidation. How might this happen?

When you filled out your consolidation paperwork, you didn't list one or more of your loans. You may have forgotten about one or more of your loans or didn't know about them, or you compiled the list of student loans from your paperwork for the loans you know about and are making payments on, but forgot one of your bills.

The other way you could end up with one loan outside of consolidation is through computer or human error. Double-check all of your paperwork before consolidation. Also follow up with the new servicer within a week or two of consolidating to make sure they show all of your loans included in the process.

You may be able to catch the stray loan and get it into the consolidation before the consolidation is complete. But if you don't, you can reconsolidate your loans, as discussed in the next section.

Checklist for Corralling Stray Loans

✓ Before you start the consolidation process, check the student loan database and/or your credit reports to make sure you've included all your loans.

✓ Double-check all forms before you submit them.

✓ Follow up with your servicer and go over loans one-by-one to make sure all loans were included in your new consolidation loan.

✓ If you catch a mistake, follow up with your new servicer immediately to correct it.

✓ If it's too late, you should reconsolidate the missing loan in with your consolidation loan.

Reconsolidating

Your eyes absolutely pop out of your head when you read over your Loans chart from the National Student Loan Database and you realize you consolidated and reconsolidated four times! What does this mean, how did this happen, could you do it again if you so desired, and could you get a better deal?

This is actually my situation. I consolidated my loans four different times. The first time was for my initial undergraduate loans. The second time was to include loans from when I returned to school to include the remainder of my undergraduate degree. Then I did a mini-consolidation of two loans right before an interest rate hike was expected in order to fix the rate—this was before each federal student loan started being issued at fixed interest rates. The final reconsolidation was right after graduation for my first master's to secure one of the consolidation benefits before they ended in October 2007. I could still reconsolidate one more time with direct loans, if the current program or a program ten years from now with direct loans seems more beneficial for paying off my loan faster.

Why might you want to reconsolidate?

If you decided to work for the government or a nonprofit business, you could get on a plan where the rest of your loan would be forgiven after 120 payments on specific plans such as income-based repayment while working in a public service position for ten years. It would also be a good option if you returned to school and wanted one uniform payment. If you missed a loan and didn't want to lose out on benefits earned from a previous consolidation, this is not a time to reconsolidate—at least until your benefit is earned.

Note: Loans made on or after July 1, 2010, are automatically direct loans. Thus, on these loans you wouldn't need to consolidate them to get on public service loan forgiveness.

There's another situation where reconsolidation could be a good idea: You consolidated before October 2007 with a consolidation benefit of a 2 percent interest rate deduction after 36 on-time payments and your new interest rate is secured for the life of your loan. You'd rather have your consolidation loan with direct lending to make sure your loan is never sold to another bank.

No matter what your situation is, weigh your options carefully and reconsolidate when you are able to and when it makes sense for your individual circumstances.

Checklist for Reconsolidating

✓ Review your current consolidation terms before doing any reconsolidating.

✓ Before you fill out an online form perform the calculations to make sure reconsolidating is beneficial for your situation.

✓ If you qualify for a rebate or interest rate reduction, wait to reconsolidate until you've qualified for your consolidation benefit. Then, you can reconsolidate and keep your same interest rate.

✓ Keep in mind that reconsolidating doesn't make sense for everybody. Do it if you qualify for some benefit through the government, such as public service loan forgiveness.

Chapter Wrap-Up

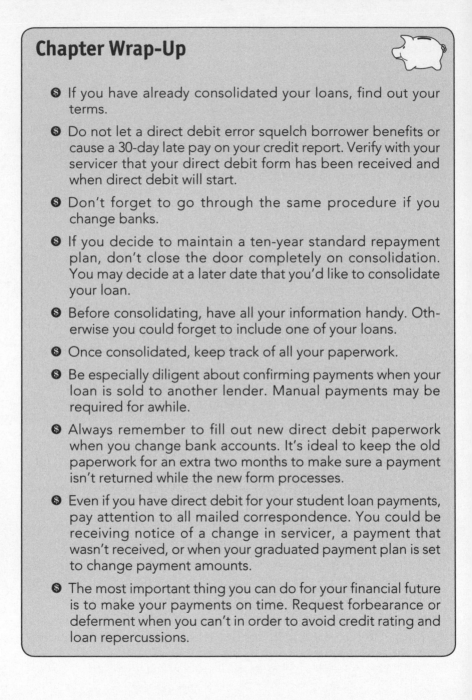

- ⑤ If you have already consolidated your loans, find out your terms.

- ⑤ Do not let a direct debit error squelch borrower benefits or cause a 30-day late pay on your credit report. Verify with your servicer that your direct debit form has been received and when direct debit will start.

- ⑤ Don't forget to go through the same procedure if you change banks.

- ⑤ If you decide to maintain a ten-year standard repayment plan, don't close the door completely on consolidation. You may decide at a later date that you'd like to consolidate your loan.

- ⑤ Before consolidating, have all your information handy. Otherwise you could forget to include one of your loans.

- ⑤ Once consolidated, keep track of all your paperwork.

- ⑤ Be especially diligent about confirming payments when your loan is sold to another lender. Manual payments may be required for awhile.

- ⑤ Always remember to fill out new direct debit paperwork when you change bank accounts. It's ideal to keep the old paperwork for an extra two months to make sure a payment isn't returned while the new form processes.

- ⑤ Even if you have direct debit for your student loan payments, pay attention to all mailed correspondence. You could be receiving notice of a change in servicer, a payment that wasn't received, or when your graduated payment plan is set to change payment amounts.

- ⑤ The most important thing you can do for your financial future is to make your payments on time. Request forbearance or deferment when you can't in order to avoid credit rating and loan repercussions.

Managing Your Private Loans and Payoff Strategies

If part—or all—of your student loan debt consists of private student loans, you are not alone. Private student loan lending is a multi-billion-dollar industry. And because these loans—unlike federal loans—are granted and assigned variable rates based on credit ratings, often a co-signer to the loan can be held responsible for loan repayment.

But what does all this mean to you in your personal battle against student debt? Plenty. If you have private student loan debt, you need a specialized plan of attack that starts with understanding exactly what you got yourself into when you took out these loans, including the terms of your loan, how your interest rate is calculated and can change over the years, how to consolidate or transfer your debt to another loan or a low-interest credit card, and what your co-signer's responsibilities are, if you have a co-signer.

But before you can analyze your own loans, you need to learn how private loans work, including the rules regarding temporary payment reprieves. This chapter is organized into sections that explain one part of your private loan's terms at a time.

Federal Loans vs. Private Loans

Here are the basic differences between federal and private loans:
Federal loans . . .

- Have fixed interest rates.

- Allow forbearance and deferments—temporary reprieves from making payments—for when you fall on hard times.

- Offer nationally standardized repayment terms.
- Are granted without regard to credit history.

Private loans . . .

- Have mostly variable rates but some have fixed rates.
- Offer programs for economic hardship based upon the discretion of the lender.
- Offer repayment terms that are set by individual lenders.
- Are granted and assigned interest rates based on credit ratings.

Gathering Information on Your Private Loans

If you don't know much debt you have and to whom you owe the money, there's no way to deal with it. So start now and gather all the information on your private student loans. If you happen to be organized enough to have a file containing all your student loan correspondence, pull it out. If you don't have a file, create one and put all of your student loan information into it.

But what if you're not sure how many private loans you have because you took out a new one every semester, there are at least two or three lenders involved, or you can't recall the company names? No problem. There's an easy, quick, and often free fix: Pull your credit report. Your report lists all of your debt, down to the loans you took out your first year in college, with the remaining balances posted along with your payment history.

So, how do you get your credit report for free? Go online to www.annualcreditreport.com and request reports from the three credit bureaus: Equifax, TransUnion, and Experian. You are entitled to one free report per year per bureau, and you will be able to review your full credit reports online. Make sure you print a copy to review and save the reports to a file on your computer. Before you scroll down the computer screen to see how much and to whom you owe, remind yourself that you'll start to see the balances go down once you start making payments based on your personal student loan payoff strategy. Remember to look at all three of your credit reports, because you may have a loan that reported your payment history to one but not the others.

Once you've found each loan, you're not done yet. There's also a contact information section for your creditors, including addresses and phone numbers. This will be important for the next step, in which you check your interest rates, and for repayment terms, financial hardship, and options for paying off or transferring private loan debt.

Checklist for Gathering Information

✓ Get out your file containing all your information on your private loan debt.

✓ If you don't have a file, make one. Fill it with all the information you gather on your private student loans.

✓ Go online to www.annualcreditreport.com to obtain free copies of your credit reports from Equifax, TransUnion, and Experian. Use the credit reports to find out how much you owe, to whom you owe, and how to contact your lenders.

✓ Cross-reference all three reports, just in case one of your loans only appears on one or two of your reports.

✓ If you have federal loans, keep that information in a separate file, because federal loans have different rules and contract terms.

Private Loans Chart

In order to figure out what options you have for your private loans, you need to look at all of them together in one file. The easiest way to do this is to create a chart for private loans. Remember to go through your credit reports to find any loans you may have forgotten.

For the rows, list all your private loans. For the columns, use these categories:

- **Lender's name:** The name of the bank to which you owe the money for your private loans.

- **Contact information:** The phone number for your lender.

- **Interest rate terms:** Since private loans generally do not come with fixed interest rates, you'll want to write down the exact language that is used to describe your interest rate, such as LIBOR plus 4 percent or Prime plus 1 percent. Don't worry about what these terms actually mean at this point; I'll explain them in the following section.

- **Reasons why interest rate terms can change:** Look through your promissory note for phrases such as "number of" or "missed payment." Missed payments can raise your rate. Anything like this should be included in your charts, along with the percentage by which your rate could change.

- **Notes on financial hardship rules:** Write down anything you see regarding forbearances or procedures for getting temporary payment reprieves or reductions in payments due to financial hardship.

Simply filling in this chart won't solve your private loan situation, but it will keep all your loans and information in one place for easy reference.

Interest Rate Terms

It seems like every time you make your monthly payment on your private student loans it's for a different amount. You'd love to construct a monthly budget, but you feel like your private student loan payment is on the opposing team in dodgeball, trying to duck or lunge every time you try to tag it for budget inclusion.

How do you win the budgeting game when you have a variable-rate loan that can go up and down on a regular basis? By understanding the rules of how rates can change and budgeting for a range of payments.

UNDERSTANDING YOUR RATE QUOTE

When you first applied for your private student loans, you went through a similar process as you would to apply for any consumer loan. Your credit was checked, and you had to disclose your income. If you couldn't qualify on your own, a co-signer was required—probably your mom, dad, or another relative who would soon become your favorite for helping you get the money you needed for your education.

Based on your credit—or your co-signer's—you were assigned interest rate terms. Notice I said interest rate *terms* instead of an interest rate. An interest rate is something you get with a fixed-rate loan or a loan that is fixed for a period of time of a year or more. For variable-rate loans, your interest rate is based on an economic index, normally LIBOR or Prime, which I'll tell you more about in a moment. The index acts as a basis for helping the bank figure out how much it will cost them to borrow the money they need to lend to you.

"Banks just stand in the middle," says Dr. James Conover, finance professor at the University of North Texas. Banks borrow the funds that they lend out, which changes in cost for the banks every night. How often your rate changes based on the index depends on your loan. You could have a loan based on a 1-month, 3-month, or 6-month index. However, your loan could be based on one of these indexes but change based on the terms the lender assigns in your contract. For example, a loan that is tied to the 1-month LIBOR index could change quarterly. This just means that your lender looks at the 1-month index every three months and assigns the indexed portion of your interest rate accordingly.

With the indexes changing constantly due to the state of the economy and the overall loan market, the margin—the extra interest paid—on top of the index remains stable based on your or your co-signer's credit rating. This accounts for the risk to the bank of lending to you. For example, you could have a rate of 1-month LIBOR plus 4 percent if you have a phenomenal credit rating from the same bank that gives your buddy with not-quite-as-good-credit interest rate terms of 1-month LIBOR plus 10 percent.

WHAT ARE YOUR TERMS?

Before I discuss planning for future rates and increases, you need to know your interest rate terms to be able to act on this information. If you don't remember your terms, that's why you made the Private Loans chart discussed earlier in the chapter. If you haven't completed the chart, do so now with the information from your promissory note. I'll wait for you. If you can't find the promissory note, call your lender to send you a copy. If the customer service agent is willing to fax or e-mail it to you, you can get back to this chapter faster.

LIBOR AND PRIME RATE INDEXES

As I've mentioned, the two indexes used as a basis for your student loans are LIBOR and Prime. LIBOR (London Interbank Offered Rate) is the actual rate that many banks pay to borrow money on a short-term basis, such as when you see a 1-month or 3-month LIBOR rate. When you look at the historic and current LIBOR index rates on the Federal Reserve Web site, you'll notice the different lengths of time such as one month or three months. This is because a bank may borrow the money for loans for different time periods with the rate only being effective for that time period. So, if you have a rate that is linked to the 1-month LIBOR index, your rate could change for the bank every month.

Let's look at an example of how your rate changes. Say your interest rate terms are 1-month LIBOR plus a margin of 4 percent. The 1-month LIBOR rate could be 2 percent. Your interest rate for the term your bank gives you this rate (your lender could set the interest rates to change every month, three months or six months) would be 6 percent (4 percent plus 2 percent). The next month the 1-month LIBOR rate is 2.5 percent. If the terms of your loan allow for monthly rate adjustments, your interest rate for this month would be 6.5 percent (4 percent plus 2.5 percent).

As you can see, the LIBOR-based portion of your interest rate changes, but your margin stays static. Monthly Prime rates work the same way. However, where Prime and LIBOR differ is that Prime is based on the absolute best rate lenders give their premium clients. The index is based on a survey of the Prime rates from large banks. Because it is a rate given to premium clients instead of the rate the bank is actually paying, typically the Prime index is a couple of percentage points higher than the LIBOR index.

CALCULATING YOUR FUTURE PAYMENT

In order to factor your private student loan payment into your budget, you need to find a way to estimate what your future payments will be beyond at least the next reset period of one, three, or six months. Since your interest rate goes up and down, you can't just input a monthly payment into your bill pay and be done with it. But you can budget an amount based on the highest your loan rate could get. And when your rate doesn't reach the upper echelons of your interest rate range, you can use that extra money for other things, such as increasing your emergency fund or paying down your car loan.

There's only one problem with this plan: Unless you have a time machine handy to fly 15 to 30 years into the future to check out all the ups and down of the financial indexes for the life of the loan, you really won't know how high your interest rate will rise. However, you can look back at history to see how rates have varied in the past. The following table shows a sample period of 20 years from 1977 to 1997 for both LIBOR and Prime.

Year	1-Month LIBOR Annualized	Prime
1977	5.75	6.83
1979	11.66	12.67
1981	16.72	18.87
1983	9.38	10.79
1985	8.12	9.93
1987	6.88	8.21
1989	9.16	10.87
1991	5.81	8.46
1993	3.07	6.00
1995	5.86	8.83
1997	5.52	8.44

Based on data from www.federalreserve.gov

As you can see, your interest rate can fluctuate quite a bit. But the most important part of this example is the increase in the indexes between 1979 and 1981: about 5 percent for LIBOR and about 6 percent for Prime. This two-year variance will help you determine an approximate interest rate range two years at a time.

Get out your monthly bill statement, look at your private student loan accounts online, or call your lender for the following information: your current interest rate, your current balance you have left on your loan, and the number of months you have left on your loan repayment. Add 5 percent to your current interest rate if you have a LIBOR-based loan, or add 6 percent to your current interest rate if you have a Prime-based loan. Then go to www.fico.com and use the loan calculator to calculate what your payment would be with this potential higher interest rate. This will be the amount you factor into your monthly budget. You may never pay this amount, but you won't be caught off guard if it happens.

Redo this calculation every year. Put it in your organizer or set up an e-card to remind you of the date for your yearly student loan interest rate review. You can also ask your lender to do this calculation for you.

HOW YOUR INTEREST RATE TERMS CAN CHANGE

Your rates can change based on such circumstances as missed payments on your private student loan, depending on the terms in your promissory note. Look for these terms and make a note on your Private

Loans chart. If you think you will have difficulty making the payments, contact your lender to discuss payment arrangements before it becomes a problem.

Checklist for Interest Rate Terms

✓ Because most private loans have variable rates, your loan most likely does. Find out what your interest rate terms are now by combing through your paperwork, viewing your account online, or contacting your lender.

✓ Contact your private student loan company or companies for missing or lost contracts, for recent bills, or for your interest rates.

✓ Include your interest rate terms in your Private Loans chart.

✓ Base your budgeting on a payment for a rate that is 5 percent higher than your current rate if you have a LIBOR-based loan, or 6 percent higher if you have a Prime-based loan. You'll be prepared for higher interest rates and payments. If your rate doesn't go up that much, you'll have built a hefty emergency fund off of the difference.

Debunking Private Loan Repayment Myths

Not sure if your interest rate terms could change if you miss a payment or what your options are with private loans when you encounter a financial hardship? Sallie Mae's Patricia Nash Christel and Martha Holler correct some of the most common myths surrounding private loan repayment.

Myth: Interest rates increase if you miss a payment.

Fact: There's some variance from lender to lender as to whether you will incur an interest rate hike if you miss payments. However, late fees are fairly standard. For us, the variable interest-rate terms that you qualified for when you first signed up are the variable interest terms you have for the life of your loan. For example, if you secured a rate with us of the 1-month LIBOR index plus 4 percent five years ago, you still would have a rate of LIBOR plus 4 percent five years later, even if you miss a payment.

Myth: There's only one way to repay private loans.

Fact: We and others in the industry have tried to mirror the flexibility of federal loans on the private loan side of our business. We offer graduated payment plans where you make interest-only payments for a set period of time, and extended repayment terms to extend the standard private loan term from 15 to 25 or 30 years. While this option is fairly standard for us, always check with your lender on these or any other terms of your loan.

Myth: There isn't a maximum interest rate that could be charged on your loan.

Fact: The interest rate that is charged on your loan changes based on the underlying index (such as Prime rate or LIBOR), subject to the consumer credit laws on a state-by-state basis, as well as the terms listed in your promissory note that you signed when you took out the money. Pay close attention to what your terms are in your contract.

Myth: Private loans are always more expensive to repay than federal loans.

Fact: While Sallie Mae always advises families who need to borrow to consider federal student loans first, your private loan isn't necessarily more expensive for you. For instance, let's say you took out a private loan and a federal loan in August 2006. Your federal loan was issued with a fixed rate of 6.8 percent. On July 22, 2009, the 1-month LIBOR index was at 0.28. Thus, the interest rate for private loans was cheaper for this month if you secured a rate of the 1-month LIBOR index rate plus 4 percent. However, the average LIBOR index rate since August 2006 has been 1.75 (rounded to the nearest quarter percent), which would have given you an average interest rate of 5.75 (rounded to the nearest quarter percent) percent if you secured interest rate terms of LIBOR plus 4 percent.

Myth: There's no difference between federal and private loans.

Fact: If you return to school and need to borrow, exhaust federal loan borrowing first, and then fill any tuition gap with private student loans. Federal student loans offer many features you are entitled to, such as economic hardship deferment or fixed interest rates, that make them more desirable than typical consumer debt. Private education loans offer flexibility for students as well. Whether or not you are returning to school, avoid switching federal loans to other sources such as bank loans or credit cards.

Myth: You have nowhere to go when you have trouble making a payment.

Fact: Especially during tough economic times, lenders want to work with you to help you get back on track. If you are facing financial difficulty, our procedure is to chat with you so we can understand your individual financial circumstances. If forbearance—taking a temporary break from payments for a short period of time—is an option, you may need to submit an application or send in documents to support your financial hardship. When your situation improves, you will want to go back to making full payments as soon as possible to shorten the time frame and lessen the total cost over the life of the loan.

Myth: Your loan balance can never get larger than your principal balance.

Fact: You can have negative amortization—your loan grows larger than when you started. How does this happen? If you defer making interest payments while you are in school, your balance grows. This also happens when you temporarily stop or reduce your payments. You can prevent negative amortization by making at least interest-only payments while in school and staying on track with your payment plan after school. Be sure to make extra payments when possible.

Myth: Shopping rewards earned through Sallie Mae's Upromise program only apply to federal loans.

Fact: The Upromise rewards you earn can be directly transferred toward eligible Sallie Mae-serviced private loan and federal loan accounts.

Myth: You should wait until you encounter a problem making payments before you contact your lender.

Fact: Call your lender immediately. You can find out about options you have that could make repayment easier now and in the event of a financial hardship situation. Once you know all your terms and ask questions of your lender(s), you can start thinking about accelerating your payment schedule. If you are ever in a position to make an extra payment or add an extra couple of dollars to your payment, do it. Money that isn't counted on for your everyday budget is ideal. Get some extra cash for loan repayment from sources such as tax refunds or reimbursements of money you already spent on work expenses.

Myth: All private student loans have variable interest rates.

Fact: Many private lenders are now offering fixed-rate student loans.

Myth: You're stuck with a cosigner forever.

Fact: Sallie Mae has an option where cosigners can be removed from private student loans after 12 on-time payments and passing a credit check.

Bottom line: Private loans do have different terms than federal loans, but it doesn't mean you are dealing with a loan that has no options when it comes to choosing payment plans or temporarily suspending or reducing your payments. The best weapon you have in any student loan battle is to know all your terms and to call your lender when you have questions.

Length of Repayment

You've been making payments on your private loans on time, for eight years—surely you must be close to getting your loans paid off! Not necessarily. You could have a 15- or even 30-year loan.

Equally as important as your interest rate terms is the length of your repayment period, in terms of how long it takes you to pay off your loan—and at what cost. You need to know if your loans require you to make payments for 1, 5, 15, or even 30 years. Check your contract or call your loan company to find out what your repayment terms are. But don't rely on what is said over the phone alone. Most likely you will be given accurate information regarding the term length and late fee rules, but you don't want to risk it. A customer service associate could accidentally misstate something. Have your lender fax or mail you the contract, so you know exactly what your terms of loan repayment are. Also, by having the terms in writing, you don't have to worry about forgetting or confusing what was said to you over the phone when you're overloaded with the terms of three or more different bank loans.

Keep in mind that if you didn't make your payments for a period of time during the course of your repayment term, interest still accrues without a payment being made to counteract it. Late fees may have also been charged. Thus, your repayment period may also have been extended. If you are in a situation where you are behind on your payments, ask your loan company how long it would take to repay the loan if your payments stayed on course. Use the following checklist to find out what you should ask your loan company to see when your loan will actually be paid off if you make all your payments on time from this point forward.

Here are some questions to ask your lender regarding repayment periods:

- How long is your current repayment period?
- How long was it originally?
- How did late fees and interest rate hikes alter the length of repayment in the past?
- How long could it alter repayment in the future?
- Where are the repayment rules located in the contract? Do you have a copy of the rules you can send me?

Financial Hardship

When you called up Direct Lending because you were having trouble paying your federal loans, you most likely were asked a few questions and then you were offered forbearance for a few months or even a year. You will still owe the interest, but you get a break from making payments to catch up on your other bills, possibly pay down your high-interest credit card debt, or find a new job if you lost your old one.

However, if you made the same call to a private student loan lender, you would probably not have the same ease in postponing payments. While private loans can be deferred while you are in college—with interest still accruing—there aren't mandatory rules for helping you get through a job loss, pay cut, family crisis, or health issue. There also isn't an income-based repayment plan like there is for federal student loans.

So what happens when you are in a difficult financial situation and don't want your interest rates to rise, or worse, have your wages garnished?

The good news is that many companies do work with borrowers on repayment, especially during tough times when the sheer numbers of borrowers experiencing financial hardship demand it. It's likely that you could get private loan forbearance, if the company you chose offers it, for a few months or a year. A temporary reduced payment schedule based on your financial circumstances may be available as well.

If you have a mix of private and federal student loans, also consider getting forbearance on your federal loans when you are in a financial bind. This will allow you to make payments on your private loans that may have less flexibility than your federal loans do for financial hardship situations.

The bottom line is that you won't know what your options are unless you read your paperwork and ask questions. In other words, think of a financial hardship situation as if you were taking one of your tougher college courses. You sit in the back of the class and never ask any questions. You're having trouble, but you never ask your professor about the material you don't understand. You end up flunking the course. However, if you'd asked a few questions during class you could have come out with a good grade. Dealing with a financial hardship situation when you have private student loans is the same way. Study up, ask questions, and you'll get through it.

Checklist for Dealing with Private Loans When Experiencing Financial Hardship

✓ Whether or not you already have a problem, ask your lender what would happen if you were to experience financial hardship.

✓ Read your paperwork, but more importantly, call your loan company and see if they will work with you, since you intend to repay your loan when your financial situation improves.

✓ Don't assume you have the same options for dealing with financial hardship as with a federal student loan, but don't assume you have no options, either. Read your original promissory note for the rules regarding your loan. Have a copy sent to you if you don't know where you put it.

Options for Paying Off or Transferring Private Loan Debt

You currently have five different private loans that you took out during different semesters. Each one has different interest rate terms. Should you leave your loans as is, consolidate them, transfer part to a credit offer with a low rate for a set period of time, or focus extra money in your budget toward paying off the smallest loan amount or the highest interest rate first?

There's no one answer. It depends on your situation and on such factors as your job, your credit rating, how well you can remember to make five separate payments, and whether you will be buying a home in the near future.

Don't worry. No matter what your current situation is, you'll have a good start in figuring out what you need to do by reading and following the steps listed in this section.

CREDIT CARD TRANSFER OFFERS

If you have great credit, take advantage of it. Have you seen any 0 percent for 12 months or 4.9 to 6.9 percent offers on credit cards for the life of your loan in your mailbox lately? Transfer as much as you can to one of these cards to save on interest accrued. However, there are some cautions that you should heed:

- Don't transfer any more to a 12-month offer than you can reasonably pay off in a year because your interest rate will increase afterward on the remaining balance of what you transferred to your credit card. For example, if you have $300 left over at the end of each month after putting away money for savings, then you can transfer $3,600 to a credit card on a 12-month offer at 0 percent. If you opt for the 12-month offer, go to your bank's Web site and use the simple loan calculator to calculate what balance you could afford with a $300-per-month payment.

- Budget so that you can make payments on the private loan balance you weren't able to transfer at the same time as your credit card payments. You don't want your plan to save you money in interest but cost you a bundle in late fees for delayed payments while you shuffle your debt to make your regular payments on your loan. Remember, no matter how much you transfer of your private loan, your payment may not drop proportionately. This is because while the principal on your loan drops, you could have your variable interest rate on your private loan rise the next month.

- When budgeting to see how much you could afford to pay off through a balance transfer, don't use your current month's payment. If your interest rate on your private loans rises, you could throw your entire budget out of whack. Remember how your interest rate terms work and calculate what your payment would be if your interest rate jumped 5 percent for a LIBOR-based loan or 6 percent for a Prime-based loan.

- Know what your balance transfer fees are. You won't do yourself any good unless you know exactly what you are paying. For instance, let's say your 0 percent interest offer comes with a balance transfer fee of 4 percent. If you transfer $5,000, you're charged $200 right off the bat to borrow the money. This is equivalent to the interest you would pay in one year to pay off $5,000 at 7.31 percent interest. Unless your terms currently produce an interest rate that is more than this, you shouldn't be doing a balance transfer. Always compare the interest that would be charged to the balance transfer fee. Using a simple loan calculator on your bank's Web site, enter your current interest rate with the amount you want to borrow and 12 months. If this number is lower than your balance transfer fee, you may not want to do the balance transfer at this time. If it's within $20 or $30, you may want to do it just to secure a fixed interest rate on part of your loan.

- If you plan on buying a home in the near future, only transfer enough that you won't go over 15 percent of your credit limit on your card. This is because your credit score is partially determined by the percentage of your available credit that is used. Getting a lower interest rate on part of your loan won't help you if it affects whether you qualify for a home loan.

CONSOLIDATION

Just like federal loans, your private loans can be consolidated. Similar to federal loans, consolidation will streamline your payments into one payment for all your private loans, and reduce the amount you pay each month because your repayment period will be stretched out over a longer term.

Where your private loans differ is that your new interest rate terms may not have anything to do with your previous interest rate terms. This is because federal loan consolidation rates are merely the average rate of your federal loans you are consolidating. (Note that since all federal consolidation loans have fixed interest rates, I refer to these loans as having interest *rates* instead of interest rate *terms*.)

When refinancing a private loan, you'll get new interest rate terms based on what is currently being offered, and your credit and payment history will likely be reconsidered. The bright side is that you can get quotes from different loan companies, just as you would if you were refinancing a mortgage. Also, if your credit has improved since you originally borrowed your loan, you could get better terms or no longer need to have a co-signer. For example, let's say you currently have $60,000 in private loans with terms of 1-month LIBOR plus 10 percent. Your credit has improved, and you can now get terms of 1-month LIBOR plus 4 percent. The 6 percent difference in your margin could save you up to $300 a month on your extended 30-year loan versus an extended plan at your old terms. The money you'd save is regardless of how much your interest rate might vary.

Do Your Homework

How do you find the right bank and the best deal when refinancing your loan? Here are some tips:

- Don't limit yourself to your current lenders. With a private loan, you can call up any bank that offers private consolidation loans to get a quote. Start by calling your current lenders, then your current bank, and then perform an online search for private consolidation loans. Get at least three different quotes.

- If you are considering consolidating, make a photocopy of your Private Loans chart that you created earlier in this chapter. Then on the photocopy add rows to the chart. Add a column for origination fees, too. This way you can compare them on one sheet of paper.

- Especially if one of your quotes comes from a bank you've never heard of, search the Internet for positive and negative reviews.

- Pay attention to both the margin and the index. For instance, you don't want to sign up for a Prime rate loan with the same margin added to it as a LIBOR-based loan. Historically the difference between the two could be 2.5 percent to 3 percent.

What to Ask

Here are some questions you should be sure to ask lenders before consolidating:

- Is there a loan origination fee? A loan origination fee means the lender will charge you a percentage of your loan when you take out your new consolidation. For example, if you owe $60,000 and the loan origination fee is 1 percent, you will be charged $600 for the consolidation. Sometimes a loan origination fee can be worth it. For example, let's say in your consolidated loan, the margin portion of your interest rate terms is 1 percent lower. You would pay $600 to consolidate your loans, but would save $600 this year and 1 percent of the balance each following year.

- Will you consolidate loans from other banks? If you have loans from more than one lender, you want to ask each new lender you are considering if they will also take on your other private loans.

- How long is the new repayment period? You need to know just how long it will take you to repay the loan with your extended repayment period.

> ### Caution
>
> Never consolidate federal loans with private loans. You don't want to lose your federal loans' fixed interest rates and special repayment options.

- What circumstances will cause a change in the interest rate, such as a late or missed payment? How much would your interest rate increase in this situation?

REFOCUSING YOUR BUDGET

How do you squeeze more cash out of your budget to pay off your private student loans faster? By refocusing your budget toward paying off your private loans first. (Needless to say, if you have credit cards with higher rates, those should be your first priority.)

So, how do you refocus your budget?

- If you have a few dollars left at the end of the month, put that cash toward your private student loan debt instead of fixed-rate car loans or federal student loans. The less money you are loaned at a variable rate, the better.

- Even adding $5 or $10 will help toward paying off your loan, but don't refocus your budget so much that you end up paying late fees on other loans or having no cushion in your savings or checking accounts.

- Put part or all of any workplace bonuses or tax refunds toward paying your loans.

Checklist for Transferring or Paying Off Your Private Loans

✓ Don't do anything that would prevent you from paying your current private loan payments and mandatory bills on time.

✓ Since private loans are not guaranteed by the government, private loan companies have to rely on credit ratings to evaluate whether you will pay the loan back and what interest rate to assign to the loan. Thus, it's best to consolidate only when your credit rating has improved or interest rates have improved.

✓ Compare the quotes of at least three banks when deciding whether to consolidate your loan. Pay attention to both the index used and the margin offered. Don't forget to also ask about loan origination fees.

✓ If you are going to transfer part of your loan to a credit card, evaluate the interest rate terms. Don't transfer more than what would put your balance at more than 15 percent of your credit limit. For example, if your credit card has a maximum credit limit of $5,000, don't transfer more than $750. You also shouldn't transfer more than what you can pay off during the balance transfer promotion period.

Case Study: Repaying $300,000 in Student Loan Debt

Kristen and her husband Erik manage their money so well that they could be role models for financial good sense. They see their student loans payments as their number-one priority. Other than going out a couple of times per month, their only luxury expense was their gym membership—and they recently traded in that expense for home workout equipment, saving them 75 percent on their fitness bill.

They have $300,000 in student debt—50/50 federal and private loans—but they managed for the first couple of years to remain on a 15-year payment plan for their private loan debt and the standard 10-year plan for their federal student loans. Their payments take up more of their income than car payments, rent, food, clothing, and all other expenses combined.

Kristen says, "We don't really budget for our debt—we just think of student loans essentially like two more rent payments on top of our initial rent payment."

But no matter how well they handle their money, they would have difficulty getting a mortgage with their high debt-to-income ratio (the amount of their income that goes toward debt payments). Having children has also been postponed for a few years. It's as if their life is on hold.

What can this couple do to fix their debt-to-income ratio problem?

First, they have to accept an extended payment plan—and not feel defeated by it. It was really hard for them to even consider a longer payment plan because it felt like they were making their loan repayment into a permanent situation. But it actually allows the banks to see them as having less required money going out each month. However, they can still make the same payment they made before extending their plan. If they choose to do that, they can pay off their loan in the same amount of time with the same payment they made before, but choose to put the difference in savings.

Next, Kristen and Erik have to concentrate on building enough in savings to put down at least 10 percent on the home they want. With lower student loan payments, they'll be able to save a few hundred dollars a month. They are also using TurboTax to amend two years of tax returns to declare their student loan interest deduction. This wasn't done when they originally filed their taxes because they didn't know they could do so without itemizing deductions.

How much could filing amended returns help them toward their financial goals? By declaring their student loan deduction for their last tax year, they received an extra $1,000 on their tax refund that can go toward their down payment on a home.

Between the refunds they've already received and the savings from using lamps and halogen light bulbs instead of track lighting, in a few months they were able to put $3,000 into savings. Within a few years, they will own their first home and have a healthy savings account to boot.

Here are a few lessons we can learn from Kristen and Erik's triumphs and struggles:

- **Any amount of debt can be manageable.** If Kristen and Erik can find a way to make payments on $300,000 in student debt, the rest of us can find a budget that will work for us. (For budgeting help, see Chapter 5, "Budgeting for Your Lifestyle and Your Loans.")

- **If you need to extend your payment plan, don't feel bad about it.** Extending your payment plan makes you a better risk for banks afraid you won't be able to make mortgage payments because of too great a monthly debt load. You can always add money to your reduced payment when you have extra cash available.

- **File amended returns if you didn't declare your student loan interest deduction or education tax credits.** There could be thousands waiting for you—a nice chunk of money you can put toward a down payment on your first home or paying off your loans early.

- **If you return to school, watch every borrowed dollar.** If Kristen and Erik could do it all over again, they say they would have considered going to a public law school, which would have eliminated over $200,000 in student debt. Think carefully about your future student loan payments when making any choices about additional degrees.

The Debt-to-Income Ratio for Private Loan Debt

Your private student loan debt is expensive, but sometimes focusing your money on paying off private student loan debt first goes against the primary purpose of this book, which is to manage your student debt in a way that allows you to still live your life now. This is because your debt-to-income ratio could be too high.

How can paying your private student loan off quicker cause a problem for living your life now?

Lenders for homes and some car loans look at your income compared to your debt load—all your payments—to see if you can afford to take on more debt (such as a mortgage or a vehicle loan payment). While working toward paying off a private student loan early will make your debt shrink, you are still going to have close to the same payment for the near future that is part of your debt-to-income ratio calculation.

A desirable debt-to-income ratio for home lenders is 41 percent. Your debt-to-income ratio is your total debt payments divided by your monthly income. Your debt payments include minimum credit card payments, car and other vehicle loan payments, and student loan payments. To evaluate whether you meet the debt-to-income requirements, your lender will also factor in your potential mortgage, property taxes, and home insurance in the debt part of your equation.

For example, let's say your gross income is $60,000 per year, which comes out to $5,000 per month. Forty-one percent of $5,000 equals $2,050. Now let's say these are your monthly bills:

Credit card minimum payments total: $300

Car loan payment: $300

Current private loan payment: $500

Current federal loan payment: $425

Sample debt-to-income ratio:

($300 + $300 + $500 + $425) ÷ $5,000 = 30.5 percent (multiply by 100 to get 30.5 percent)

That's before any mortgage, home insurance, property tax expenses, or homeowner's association dues (if applicable). If you subtract 30.5 percent from a desirable debt-to-income ratio of 41 percent, you have 10.5 percent of your income left for a mortgage payment and other expenses in owning a house. In this case, 10.5 percent × $5,000 = $525. With a 6 percent interest rate, you'd qualify for approximately a $61,000 30-year mortgage—which wouldn't get you much in just about any housing market. (This number factors in a property tax estimate of 1 percent per year and homeowner's insurance of $1,000 per year. This figure could change based on differences in either of these numbers or if the home you choose requires homeowner's association dues, or a low down payment could require buying private mortgage insurance, PMI. This is a loan value, so a down payment would increase the value of the home you could buy by the amount you put down.)

What could you do to make your debt-to-income ratio more attractive to lenders?

- **Consolidate or extend your federal loan payment.** In the previous example, this person had $40,000 worth of federal loans on a ten-year payment plan at 5 percent interest. After two years of making monthly payments of $425 on her federal loan, her loan balance is $33,512. If she consolidated the remainder of her loan into a new loan for 20 years, her new payment would be $221.16. The extra $204 would decrease her debt-to-income ratio by 4.1 percent and give her an extra $204 a month to pay toward her mortgage. She could pay more on the loan when she can. Unlike her private loan, she won't have to worry about her rate adjusting during the longer time period.

- **Pay off or pay down credit cards and car loans.** This a good thing for your debt and your debt-to-income ratio. Pay off the credit card with the smallest balance first and work your way up. In the previous example, getting rid of credit card debt would cut her debt-to-income ratio by 6 percent. However, if her minimum payments were calculated based on $300 being 4 percent of her overall balance, her total credit card debt is $7,500. Let's say she had only $3,000 left on her car loan. If she paid off her car loan, she'd decrease her debt-to-income ratio by 6 percent and have $300 extra every month to pay toward her mortgage and now can possibly afford a condo in some home markets. By combining this with some of the other changes, she could afford and qualify for a very nice home.

> ## Caution
>
> When paying extra on any debt payment—or taking on new debt like a mortgage—make sure you can afford it. One of the worst things you can do is try to move ahead financially only to end up making late payments or not being able to pay your current obligations.

If you can improve your debt-to-income ratio, should you buy a home? Once you get your debt-to-income ratio down to where you can qualify for a home if you have a good credit rating, you need to make sure you can afford all of the expenses involved in homeownership, including a mortgage, property taxes, repairs, and utility bills. You should also plan on being in your home for at least five years, because homes can take a long time to sell and occasionally can go down in value. If you love your home and are planning on living in it for a long time, you can weather anything that happens in the housing market.

Ask yourself the following questions:

- Am I willing to practice making mortgage, property tax, and home insurance payments by putting in my savings account the remainder of what I'm willing to spend on a home beyond my current rent?

- Would I still have enough left over in my budget if my private loan's interest rate went up by 5 percent?

- Have I considered expenses for repairs and the utility cost for the size of home I want?

- After I work toward paying off credit cards and car/vehicle loans, will I have enough left over to save for a down payment?

- Do I like the area enough that I wouldn't mind if at some point my property value dipped, because I'm committed to living here for at least five years?

If you aren't sure how your budget could handle paying down your credit cards and paying off your car loan early, check out Chapter 5 on budgeting.

Checklist for Debt-to-Income Ratios When You Have Private Loan Debt

✓ Get out your bills and add up all your current debt payments. Then divide this number by your monthly gross income.

✓ Consolidate federal loans with other federal loans in order to reduce your debt load.

✓ Pay off credit card and car loans first as you are able.

Should You Choose Fixed-Rate Private Loans if Returning to School?

Since the first edition of *Graduation Debt* published, fixed-rate private student loans have entered the scene. Sometimes these loans have lower rates than federal student loans. While previously I would have said always choose federal student loans, there is a very good reason to choose private student loans with fixed interest rates: You're borrowing money for a short time period, and your payment amount won't change as interest rates fluctuate.

For instance, you're borrowing $10,000 for a master's program. You're working the whole time and will be able to repay the money within two years. Because you're going to repay the money in two years, guaranteed federal student loan benefits such as temporary repayment reprieves may not be so important. However, avoiding federal student loan origination fees and a higher interest rate are important.

This doesn't mean I'm advocating private student loans over federal student loans in general. But should you really turn down a 4 percent interest rate on a loan you can repay in two years?

Now, if you're borrowing $40,000 and you know you'll take 15 years to repay the money, borrow federal student loans. The additional repayment options will be worth it.

Checklist for Deciding Whether to Borrow Fixed-Rate Private Student Loans

- Figure out how long and how much you want to borrow.

- Compare interest rates and loan origination fees with federal student loans.

- Choose private fixed-rate student loans when you're borrowing a smaller loan amount you can repay quickly based on your current salary.

- Choose federal student loans when you don't plan on repaying the loan quickly.

Chapter Wrap-Up

- ⑤ Create a Private Loans chart with information such as final payoff amounts, maximum interest rates, and lender contact information for all of your private loans. Keep this chart in a place where you know exactly where you put it.

- ⑤ For variable rate loans, always plan on a payment that's based on an interest rate that is 5 percent higher than your current payment. Recalculate this based on the current payment every two years. This way you'll never be unprepared if your interest rate goes up.

- Go to www.annualcreditreport.com for free copies of your credit reports from Equifax, TransUnion, and Experian. Your credit reports contain balance, payment history, and contact information for all your private student loans—even those you may have forgotten you had.

- Make sure you have all the terms of your private loans in writing. This will help you not only keep track of everything you need to know about what you can expect from your lender, but if the lender raises your interest rate or adjusts your payment, you'll know why.

- Find in your contract when and why your private loan company can adjust your payments.

- Consider a fixed-rate private student loan if you are returning to school while also working full time.

- Talk to your lender when you have—or expect to have—problems making payments.

Budgeting for Your Lifestyle and Your Loans

You want your home to be a place where you can relax, not a place where you sulk about unexpected bills and the gourmet coffee drinks you're missing in order to pay your student loans. So how do you stay calm and collected when thoughts of paying for student loans, rent, utilities, and even groceries are swimming in your head?

One idea is to keep a financial diary to track what you're spending and determine how to better manage your expenses. Once you have your expenses written down in one place, you can analyze where your income is going and develop an all-inclusive budget based on your personal must-haves for spending, plus a cushion for extra expenses.

Keeping track of expenses in a financial diary for a month at a time will help you learn how to cut costs with minimal sacrifice by saving money on utilities, housing costs, groceries, and auto insurance policies, so you can afford to go out and have fun, too.

Budgeting Starts Today

Before you set off to create a financial diary, get yourself in a mindset to not judge yourself for the financial mistakes you made in the past or may be making now. The remodeling of your budget begins today.

If you get sticker shock when you find out you're actually spending $900 a month on groceries versus the $400 you budgeted for—I've pulled this one myself—figure out what's causing the extra spending and see if you were underestimating an expense you need. Was your budgeting based on wishful thinking of what you'd like your budget to be, or were you just overspending?

In the case of groceries, I've done this both ways. When I first started college and was on my own for the first time, I called my dad because I was so proud that I'd spent only $18 on groceries for the week: Ramen noodles and tuna fish. This was completely wishful thinking. No one can live on Ramen noodles and tuna alone, and pretty soon I was using credit cards to help pay for the real cost of groceries. It took a year before I learned my lesson on accurately budgeting for the real cost of groceries.

A couple years ago, before my financial "aha" moment, I was budgeting $200 a month for groceries and $100 per month for dining out. I actually spent about $400 for groceries and $150 for dining out, and the sad thing was, about $75 a month was spent on produce that ended up spoiling. I didn't make up the difference so much on credit cards, but it did deplete my resources for paying off my cards.

With a little elbow grease I got my total food budget down to $400 a month for both dining out and grocery shopping. Through careful budgeting, I've managed to keep it at that rate while living in New York City and enjoying quite a few lattes at local cafés.

Before moving, I cut my grocery budget with help from Teri Gault's thegrocerygame.com Web site, which I'll tell you about later in the chapter. I stopped buying everything that goes on sale; now I wait for the really good sales that will save me the most money on the items I eat every week, like chicken breasts. If you live in an area of the country where, like New York City, you may shop at a lot of smaller grocery stores, do what I do. I studied my neighborhood for both prices and quality of groceries. I have one store that I shop at monthly for meat and fish, one store plus farmers markets for produce, and one store conveniently located for items like eggs and milk.

I don't punish myself anymore for my past spending, just like I don't punish myself for my past credit card debt or current student loans. I focus on realizing what I'm doing now, so I can improve my financial future.

Checklist for Preparing Your Mindset to Revitalize Your Budget

✓ Don't judge yourself for your past and current spending.

✓ Understand that you will have areas where you may be spending more than you thought in certain categories, but you realize these are areas that you can improve on.

✓ Remember that budgeting is a process. Even after months of keeping a financial diary, there may still be areas that you want to adjust.

✓ Keep track of all expenses, either by writing them down in a financial diary or using an electronic format.

Create a Financial Diary

Do you remember how the paycheck from your first after-college job seemed like a mountain of money compared to the low wages you received from part-time jobs during college? You immediately treated your friends to a few drinks and fell in love with being able to afford your own place and not having to depend on your parents for emergency cash. Then reality hit—and hit hard.

Now that you are out of school, student loans are coming due. You're renting an apartment for $700, you racked up an electric bill of $100, and the phone bill adds another $100. Plus, you just received the bill from your credit card for $500 for the new clothes you bought for work. Yikes!

Whether you're still in shock over what your expenses actually are or you feel you've got everything completely under control, logging all your expenses into a financial diary never hurt anyone—and you may find expenses you never knew you had, or expenses that add to up to more than you thought. For instance, you may have counted the price of your gym membership as part of your budget, but didn't consider the price of protein shakes, smoothies, and a locker rental.

So how do you find your hidden expenses? Track everything in a financial diary for one month. No expense is bad or good, you just need to track everything. Your financial diary is a rundown of what you currently spend. It may include more or less of what you should be spending. For example, you may forget a credit card expense or have a student loan that is currently in deferment.

WRITE OUT YOUR EXPECTED BUDGET

You're absolutely positive you are already frugal with your money. You've kept track in your head, and you don't seem to be overspending on anything. Yet, somehow you've racked up $5,000 on credit cards this year alone.

You may be absolutely right that you're not being extravagant—you could have had a one-time emergency expense that caused your credit card debt. It could also be that you have a lifestyle-to-income gap where you're going out for fancy dinners every night and shopping on the weekends, or your apartment is more than you can afford on your income level.

The best way to find out if what you think you are spending is what you are actually spending is to compare your actual expenses to the expenses you expect to have every month. So before you begin your month of keeping a financial diary, fill in your monthly budget sheet with your best guess of your current spending. You can use a computerized budget sheet, or use the Monthly Budgeting Worksheet later in this chapter and fill in the Expected Expenses column.

For example, if you think you're spending $200 a month on clothing, put this number under Expected Expenses for clothing. Don't bother looking up this number on your bank account or credit card statements because it's important to learn the difference between what you *think* you are spending versus what you are *actually* spending.

Checklist for Expected Expenses

✓ Fill in your expected expenses on the Monthly Budgeting Worksheet later in this chapter or on a computerized budget sheet.

✓ Be careful not to calculate what you are spending before filling in your expected expenses. It's an important part of the process to realize the difference between what you actually spend and what you think you're spending.

PICK YOUR LOGGING METHOD FOR YOUR FINANCIAL DIARY

The first step in creating a financial diary is to decide how you are going to keep track of your expenses on a daily basis. Options include:

- **Phone:** If you're a texting wiz, plug the numbers into memos on your cell phone and e-mail it to yourself on a daily basis. Quicken Online has a free and easy iPhone application for on-the-go budgeting.

- **Memo pad:** Get a small memo pad you can put in your pocket, briefcase, or purse.

- **Journal:** Pick out an attractive journal that you'll want to bring with you wherever you go to write down your expenses throughout the day. Or use a plain spiral-bound notebook if you don't want to get that fancy.

- **Keep daily receipts in a pocket or wallet:** At the end of each day, add up all of the receipts and write down what you spent.

CATEGORIZING YOUR EXPENSES

How organized you are when you log your daily expenses is up to you. You can incorporate categories into your daily written, computerized, or cell phone expense sheets or memos. For instance, you can create a category for eating out and put your morning coffee and lunchtime soup and panini underneath. The other option is to just write down everything and save the categorizing for your monthly budget.

However, writing things down in categories can get hairy in the first few days of the exercise. Let's say you didn't think about the number of times a day you get coffee or have an unplanned night out or grocery shopping trip. Now, you have to make space for the categories you've forgot about. For this reason, you should have a miscellaneous category if you choose to categorize your daily expenses as you go.

What's eating out to one person is grocery shopping to another. For instance, you could go to a café that's part of a grocery store and get a great salad, sushi plate, or roasted chicken sandwich for lunch. If you don't grocery shop during the week, that's as close to grocery shopping as you get. Keep in mind, too, that grocery shopping isn't always done in grocery stores. Maybe you're in a rush on the way home and buy a gallon of milk at the same gas station where you filled your tank.

> **Caution**
>
> Know your limits. Certain stores —whether it's a gourmet grocery store, electronics store, or clothing boutique—may be harder to control yourself in than others. If you know you are going credit-card-first into a danger zone, either bring the cash with you that you want to spend or avoid the store altogether.

Have clear definitions of what you consider to fall into a category. Otherwise, you won't be able to keep track of differences in your expected, actual, and desired budgets accurately.

Checklist for Categorizing Expenses

✓ Use category names that make sense to you. One person's veggie burger may be totaled under Groceries; for another, it may be totaled under Dining Out.

✓ Use category names you'll remember and recognize a month later.

✓ Don't create too many or too few categories. For instance, if you have Thai food just once a month, it probably shouldn't be its own category. Put it under Dining Out instead.

TOTALING YOUR DAILY EXPENSES IN YOUR MONTHLY BUDGET

You spent $30 one day, $10 another day, and $90 another day, but what do those numbers really mean? Nothing yet. After all, you get paid on a weekly, biweekly, or monthly basis, and most of your bills are monthly, not daily. But those numbers will mean something when you add them together to find out how much you are actually spending in each category. Some of your expected expenses and actual expenses could be the same, and your difference between the two would be $0.

Listing items that are payroll deductions is optional because you never actually see the money before it is removed from your paycheck. In fact, it may be better to not include these items in your budget because then you may think about the money you are putting into your 401K or health insurance as money that could possibly be budgeted elsewhere.

Following is a worksheet that you can fill in or use for ideas for your own budget.

Monthly Budgeting Worksheet				
Expense Category	Expected Expenses	Actual Expenses	Difference	Desired Budget
Rent/mortgage				
Property tax				
Homeowners'/renters' insurance				
Home maintenance				
Home decor				
Student loan payments				
Credit cards				
Car payments				
Car maintenance				
Car insurance				
Pets				
Dining out				
Groceries				
Utilities				
Phone				

Expense Category	Expected Expenses	Actual Expenses	Difference	Desired Budget
Medical				
Health insurance				
Gas				
Clothing				
Gifts				
Investments				
Savings				
Miscellaneous				
Miscellaneous				
Miscellaneous				

Checklist for Your Financial Diary

✓ Did you include student loan payments?

✓ Did you include credit card payments?

✓ Did you include all bill payments automatically coming out of your bank account or credit cards?

✓ Did you remember all pet expenses?

✓ Did you include snacks from machines, cafeterias, or restaurants while at work?

✓ Did you include gas expenses?

✓ Did you include all communication expenses: cell phone, home phone, and Internet?

✓ Did you include continuing education or new schooling expenses?

✓ Did you include all your expenses?

Getting the Best Rate

If you've always paid the same amount for auto insurance, cable, or telephone payments, how do you know if you're overpaying? For car insurance, conduct Internet searches on sites that are Better Business Bureau (BBB)-approved, or from BBBOnline members for auto insurance quotes. There are numerous Web sites out there for comparing auto insurance rates in your area. As with anything else, get at least three comparison quotes. You can find out if a Web site is a member by looking for the BBBOnline logo on the Web site. The BBB accepts and publishes information about the complaint history for thousands of companies. Enter the name of the Web sites on which you are thinking about searching for car insurance prices into the search box at www.bbb.org to make sure the Web site has a good reputation. You should also go to your state's Department of Insurance Web site to check for a complaint history on an auto insurance company to which you are considering switching your policy. You could save hundreds of dollars a year by getting the best auto insurance rates.

Ask your cable provider or telephone company about specials. You may get free movie channels for six months or a couple of months of free cable when you bundle your telephone with your cable service from the same company. Many cable companies now provide digital phone lines and many phone companies now provide television services. Make them compete for your money by getting a quote from two or three companies, and then you'll have negotiating power.

Checklist for Comparing Auto Insurance, Telephone, and Cable Rates

✓ Don't assume your insurance rate is the lowest you can get just because it's what you've always paid.

✓ Compare at least three different insurance carriers to find out the best rate.

✓ Use a BBB-approved Web site for comparison shopping.

✓ Check your state's Department of Insurance Web site to verify low-complaint records for any auto insurance company you are considering.

✓ Ask about specials from your telephone and cable companies. Compare rates among other carriers in your area.

Saving on Groceries

When you calculated your grocery budget, was there a gap between what you thought you were spending on groceries and what you actually spent? Did you feel you could have spent less in order to afford karate lessons or to not have to put more of your monthly expenses on credit cards? Your culprit could be spoiled groceries, stock-up overload, or buying too many pricey items.

Try these tips for spending less on groceries:

- Make sure you have room in your pantry before you stock up on items.

- Don't pile anything more than two cans high, no matter how many cans you have.

- Have an organizational plan for where things like canned vegetables, pasta, and oils should go in the pantry.

- If you can't see all the way to the back of any shelf, look at what you have at the back of the shelf before you replace items you already have too many of.

- Know how much space you have in your freezer and refrigerator. It's easy to overshop when you don't know how many items your space holds. Take measurements and count items that can fit on each shelf. Write the numbers down.

- Be careful of shopping for only new recipes. Before you buy 50 different ingredients to try out in new recipes in a week, try one recipe first. You may not like how the food turns out, and you won't be disappointed if you end up not having the time to cook all the new recipes or use the items you bought. For example, you don't want to stock your pantry with Spanish or Indian spices and ingredients and then find out you really don't want to cook that kind of food as often as you thought.

Stocking up on groceries during a sale can be a smart idea. However, there are a few circumstances where it won't help in your overall budget:

- When you stock up on a different sale item every week, thus exceeding your grocery budget in the hopes of saving money in the long run.

- When you don't have room to freeze what you don't need in the next few days, and half of what should be frozen spoils.

- When you overbuy fresh fruits and vegetables and they spoil before you can use them.

- When you overstock pantry staples so that items are piled so high you can't find other items.

In addition to watching what you buy, be aware of how much you throw away. How much spoiled food do you toss out each month? If you are throwing out anything, you need to find out how much money you are wasting and nix paying for spoiled food from your budget.

Grocery-Savings Tips

Separating the facts from the myths can mean big savings on groceries. These tips are from thegrocerygame.com CEO Teri Gault, who has been clipping coupons since she was 12.

Myth: Single people and couples without kids don't need to use coupons.

Fact: Coupons have value whether they are for four people or for one person. My single friend eats the same cereal every day, but she never uses a coupon because she only shops for herself. I ask her, do you like paying full price for groceries? Buy the cereal when it's on sale. You're paying $4.85 per box when you could be paying $1.85.

Myth: Every sale is a big sale, and you should whiz through the aisles shopping for those items.

Fact: Some sales are better than others. When you use thegrocery game.com for your local grocery stores, highlight the sales that are worth an actual stock-up of an item you buy all the time. If you learn to buy on these great sales that can be 67 percent off—sometimes with a coupon, sometimes without—you'll save oodles of money and not overspend on items that you buy because of a sales tag.

Myth: Discount grocery stores are the best place to shop to spend the least amount of money.

Fact: Discount grocery stores are a great place to shop if you aren't using coupons or playing the grocery game, but there are great finds at your major local supermarket if you put in the elbow grease to save money. Normally, your major local supermarket has better sales that actually dip lower than "everyday low price" discount stores.

Myth: There's no need to buy multiples if you're single or don't have a large family.

Fact: Eighty percent of the time it will be full price if you don't. It's a good idea with health and beauty products to have at least one extra so you can always buy what you use on sale—preferably with a coupon.

Myth: If you buy multiples, you'll end up with a lot of spoilage.

Fact: To avoid spoilage, mark freezer and refrigerator items with a black marker or a label maker with the sell-by date in large, easy-to-read letters. You'll still buy produce weekly. Ask your produce manager how long the item will last in your fridge. I always talk to my produce manager about everything. I ask him to pick my cantaloupe, and tell him when I'm going to eat it. He picks just the right one to be ready on the day we want to enjoy it.

Myth: All sales are advertised.

Fact: There are great unadvertised deals to be had. On thegrocery game.com, we let you know about both unadvertised and advertised sales.

Myth: If you buy weeks in advance, you'll never find what you need in your pantry, freezer, or fridge.

Fact: Know what space you have in your pantry, freezer, and fridge and stock up accordingly. The idea is to never have to pay full price because you need stewed tomatoes for a recipe you're making tomorrow or you're completely out of your favorite cereal. You want to have a 12-week supply of what you use regularly. If space is limited, try for 6 weeks—with the notable exceptions of produce and milk. And to avoid spoilage, mark freezer and refrigerator items with a black marker or a label maker with the sell-by date or use-by date in large, easy-to-read letters.

Myth: If you wait for a good sale, you could go weeks without protein.

Fact: Every week there are two meats at your local grocery store on a terrific sale. It could be ham and fish or chicken breasts and brisket. If you eat one meat all the time, stock up when it's on super-sale, but you don't have to worry about missing out on protein in the meantime.

Myth: Bigger packages are always the better value.

Fact: Smaller packages often are a better value with a coupon because the coupon has a greater impact. One dollar off of anything in a 12-pack will net you less than a dime of savings per item, while $1 off of a 4-pack takes off 25 cents each.

Myth: Clipping coupons is tedious, time-consuming work to save pennies.

Fact: Using thegrocerygame.com, you don't have to cut and organize all your coupons. You don't even need a coupon file. Simply keep your Sunday paper inserts in a stack, putting the newest ones on top. Thegrocerygame. com will tell you which week and section to find each coupon. So now, you don't have to cut and file 150 or so coupons each week. You only cut the 20 or so you will use the week you buy the items. Mark the date with a big black marker on the front.

Myth: If you don't have time to cook, you're wasting time grocery shopping.

Fact: Most singles often eat out, get takeout, or buy convenience foods at full price more often than families. So, the cost of food for many singles is often as much as $1,000 a month, which is equal to the national average for a family of four. For singles who stock up on convenience foods and frozen meals on sale with coupons, and who are also willing to buy groceries and prepare some easy soups, chilis, and other foods that can be separated and frozen for individual meals at home, the cost of food can go down to $200 to $300 a month.

For the next month, keep a notepad in the kitchen or make a photocopy of the following table and fill it out with what you throw out and the date. At the end of the month take the list with you on your grocery shopping trip and write down the cost of each item you throw away; for example, May 12, head of lettuce, $1.29; May 17, half-pound of roast beef, $3.35.

After you write down the amount you spent on groceries that went to waste, total the amount at the bottom of the table. Think about what you could have done with this money—paid beyond the minimum on a credit card, went out to lunch an extra time, or put a few bucks toward your emergency savings.

When the exercise is complete, use the tips that follow to change your habits.

Grocery Spoilage Table		
Date Thrown Away	**Grocery Item**	**Cost**

Date Thrown Away	Grocery Item	Cost
Total Cost		

Try these tips to reduce grocery spoilage:

- Use your spoilage exercise as a lesson to buy less of what you are letting spoil. For instance, I used to buy five heads of lettuce because I hated going back to the grocery store for one thing; I would inevitably buy way more than what I came in for. Two heads always spoiled and I had to go back to the store, which took the same amount of time as if I bought three heads to begin with.

- Be honest with yourself about how often you eat out and factor it into your grocery-shopping budget. I've made the mistake of shopping for groceries as if I were going to eat every meal at home. But I always go out to eat one or two times a week, so some of that food went unused.

- Staple the Grocery Spoilage Table into your financial diary or post it on your refrigerator to remind you of what you are wasting.

- Don't put your newest grocery items in front of your older grocery items. This leads to both overstocking your refrigerator with things

> ## Caution
>
> Dry items like cake mixes and rice and pasta mixes have expiration dates, too. Go through your pantry to check the dates on the packages. Move the packages with the most recent dates to the front of the pantry so you'll remember to use them first, and throw away items that have expired.

you already have and eating the newest items first while the older items spoil.

A good resource for information on food storage and safety is nutrition.gov. Finding out the appropriate food storage times can save you from throwing out food prematurely or from buying items that will spoil before you can use them.

Prioritizing and Choosing Budgetary Cutbacks

If you are going to have to cut back on your budget, I want it to be as painless as possible. Try these ways to cut your budget with the least amount of impact on your life.

NEGOTIATING RENT

You love your apartment, but your rent takes up half your salary. Everything else in your life is starting to suffer: your social life, the fact that you're only able to make minimum payments on your credit cards, and a food budget that calls for a diet of mac and cheese and cold cuts instead of healthy produce and protein.

You're thinking about moving, but you have four months left on your lease. Plus, moving locales gets pretty pricey. Do you move now and break your lease? Do you move at the end of your lease? Or do you try to negotiate your rent with your landlord or apartment management office? If you're considering this last option, start by gathering all available information on the prices in the area and within your rental community. Most apartment communities have what is known as a market rent, which is like the retail price on a TV set, an item of clothing, or the MSRP (manufacturer's suggested retail price) on a new car. Based on how the market is doing in your area, there may be discounts or specials offered to entice new residents.

If you are renting an apartment, start talking about your rental rate with your neighbors. They may be paying less than you are, and you can use your neighbors' rate to negotiate your own.

Know what else is available in your area. Compare the features of your apartment with those of other apartments in your area. Look at the Web sites of the five closest apartment communities and call to find out their specials. Ask about specials in your own apartment complex, too. Have friends call your complex to get the newest specials for what a new resident would pay. You can use this to negotiate your rate.

If your apartment complex has a lot of empty units, this is also a good reason for your apartment management office to reconsider your rental rate. The last thing they want is to have another empty apartment when you move out. Have a friend call up to ask what their move-in specials are for new residents. There will likely be deals offered that you can mention before you sign your next lease.

Call your apartment complex with the information you have and tell them you are thinking about moving. Explain that you've heard from other residents (don't name names) that they are getting rates of x for an apartment similar to yours. Ask for a matching rate. Explore other communities if need be. Weigh your options. Will your apartment offer you a better price? If not, how much will it cost you to move? Can you afford the move? By doing the homework you may end up with a more affordable rental rate, or a brand new cozy home.

Checklist for Negotiating Rent

- ✓ Check with your neighbors for what rent they are paying for a similar apartment.

- ✓ Have friends call up your apartment complex to find out rental specials for new residents.

- ✓ Research on the Internet the rent at neighboring apartment communities.

- ✓ Consider moving if the rent can't be negotiated or is still too high for your budget.

NEGOTIATING YOUR MORTGAGE

Luckily, housing prices can also be negotiated down to a level you can afford through a loan modification (refinancing on a loan you already have) or through refinancing for a home you own. This holds true as long as your house is worth more than your loan. You can also sell your home to downsize to a smaller house you can afford.

Start by asking yourself if your payments are affordable. How does your payment relate to your income? The rule of thumb should be that your total home mortgage, home insurance, and property tax shouldn't take up more than a third of your income.

Whether or not your home is currently affordable, refinancing could lower your mortgage payment if interest rates have dropped since you bought your home. If rates have dropped at least 1 percent and you plan on staying in your home for at least five years without refinancing again, compare rates and fees among at least three mortgage brokers or banks to see where the best deal for you is.

Checklist for Negotiating Your Mortgage

✓ Make sure your home is worth more than you owe. The easiest way to do this is to go online and see what homes in your area that have similar features have sold for recently.

✓ Consider refinancing or a loan modification if market interest rates have dropped at least 1 percent from the last time you refinanced your loan.

✓ Do not refinance every other year. You'll end up with far more in fees than you'll save in interest.

✓ If your home is worth more than your mortgage but doesn't make sense for your budget and income level, consider selling it and buying a more affordable one.

> **Caution**
>
> Don't refinance just because current rates are lower than your original rate. Refinancing can be extremely expensive if you start making a habit of refinancing every time mortgage rates go down.

Negotiating Interest Rates on Debt

You can reduce your car and credit payments instantly and save money each month by negotiating interest rates. You can potentially reduce your credit interest rate by calling your credit card company and letting them know the lower interest rate of some of your other cards. You can potentially lower a car loan rate by following current market rates for auto loans and refinancing if your current rate is at least 1 percent higher than what you can get now.

How much could you save? Check out the following payment table.

Credit Card Interest Rate	Interest Charged to Borrow $2,000 for One Year	Car Loan Interest Rate	Payment on a $20,000, Five-Year Loan
8%	$160.00	0%	$333.34
12%	$240.00	4%	$368.33
16%	$320.00	6%	$386.66
20%	$400.00	8%	$405.53
24%	$480.00	14%	$465.37

Checklist for Negotiating Interest Rates on Car Loans and Credit Cards

✓ Compare your credit card interest rates. Is there one that is significantly higher than your other cards?

✓ Call your credit company and ask them to reduce your interest rate based on the lower interest rates of your other cards.

✓ Compare your auto loan to current market rates for auto loans. If your current rate is at least 1 percent higher than what you can get now, consider refinancing.

Checking Account Safety Nets

You have $5 left in your checking account until payday and you forgot that the automatic payment you set up with your utility company comes out on the 16th, regardless of the date your biweekly paycheck is direct-deposited into your account.

Luckily, your bank didn't reject your payment, but you were still charged an overdraft fee. You now have three days left until payday with a negative balance when a charge comes through for $5 from a fast-food restaurant—and you're hit with a second overdraft fee.

If you've ever felt the sting of having only $5 in your bank account until your next payday, you probably know the fear of knowing that if a direct debit or a bank charge hits, you're going to be overdrawn.

Checklist for Building a Checking Account Safety Net

✓ Before you worry about an emergency fund, start by building a safety net into your bank account in case direct debits come out early or late.

✓ Know when direct debits can be taken out. This is one of the great things about having a budget. You'll know when you have bills hitting your account and won't have to budget for overdraft fees. If you use Quicken Online, you can plug in all your bills into your budget, and it will tell you on the home screen what the risk is for a bank overdraft charge.

✓ Keep track of your paycheck arrival dates and plan your bills accordingly.

✓ To decide how much of a checking account safety net you need before you start diverting extra funds into a savings account, look at all your monthly bills for the last month and add up all the ones that are due within a two-week period or the period of one pay-check. Add in basic costs, such as for groceries.

✓ Act fast if a paycheck isn't direct-deposited on time or your check doesn't arrive when you need it. Check your account every day to make sure your payments arrived.

✓ Once you have a solid checking account safety net, begin to put aside at least $5 to $10 per month into your savings account.

Using Free Online Budgeting Tools

In the Myths and Facts below, manilla.com's Sarah Kaufman advises how to make use of free services for managing your bills and accounts online.

Myth: You can't manage non-digital accounts online.

Fact: As more and more people turn to their computers, laptops, smart-phones, and tablets to manage their bills and accounts online, compa-nies are finding solutions that allow people to virtually manage any account online. For example, you can manually add an account that you may not typically manage digitally, such as your rent, babysitter, dog walker, or local dry-cleaning service, allowing you to truly manage all of your accounts in one place.

Myth: You have to spend a fortune to earn rewards that you can track online.

Fact: Credit card and even student loan companies have rewards pro-grams that offer incentives for spending money where you already shop. For example, a credit card might offer 3 percent cash back on gas, so if you spend $200 a month on gas, you'll get $6 back on a monthly basis. It doesn't seem like a lot, but over the course of a year, you're getting almost $75 back, just for spending money on something you would have bought even without the rewards program. Another example is Upromise by Sallie Mae, a rewards program from which you can earn cash back on purchases and apply the money directly toward your student loan balance.

Myth: In order to track all of your bills and balances online, you have to log into multiple Web sites and enter multiple usernames and passwords.

Fact: One of the biggest pain points consumers face when it comes to managing all of their accounts online is that they typically have to go to multiple Web sites and enter multiple usernames and passwords. The

Auto Login feature on manilla.com allows you to access all of your provider sites to pay your bills, view account documents, and see your balances and account information with one-password access.

Myth: You don't need to budget if you don't have a lot of bills to manage.

Fact: Tracking your spending and being aware of where your money is going is essential when it comes to having a good credit score and making overall smart financial decisions. Even if you don't have a lot of bills right now, adopting responsible financial habits early on will ensure you'll have a successful financial future. For instance, if you look at your bank account, it may look like you only spend $60 on going out to eat, but you are charging another $150 on your card. If you see it in online budgeting software added together in one category, you can decide if you're happy spending $210 on dining.

Budgeting for Your Personal Must-Haves

You are trying to save, but your favorite coffee house is calling with $4 coffees. It seems like a small amount for something you love so much, but you get coffees there on average five days a week, which comes out to an $80-a-month coffee habit. Can you afford it—and will it prevent you from saving?

While personal must-haves such as your morning coffees, Friday nights at the comedy club, Saturday night dancing, or season tickets to your favorite sports team shouldn't come before rent, the phone bill, or health insurance premiums, they may be an essential part of your life. By prioritizing these items, you can have fun and stay on budget, too. In fact, if you get your essential budget items under control—such as comparing auto insurance quotes, saving money on groceries and limiting your grocery spoilage factor, and choosing housing you can afford—while enjoying a few extras, you can enjoy yourself and live within your means, too.

Next, prioritize your must-haves. List the top ten things you enjoy the most in order from 1 to 10. If you have to cut an item from your budget, you'll be able to use this list to figure out what would be the first to go in a budget crunch. Some months, depending on how the rest of your budget goes, you could afford all of these expenses and sometimes you'll just be able to afford the top half. Since your priorities could change, every few months you should construct a new list based on your current priorities.

Checklist for Budgeting for Your Personal Must-Haves

✓ Make sure you have eliminated waste from other categories so you can afford to spend money on your personal must-haves.

✓ Prioritize your personal must-haves based on what is most important to your lifestyle.

✓ Reevaluate your must-haves every few months based on your lifestyle changes.

✓ Don't spend on personal must-haves at the risk of not paying your rent, electric or phone bill, or other necessities.

Chapter Wrap-Up

Ⓢ Don't feel guilty about your past spending. You have plenty of time to rehabilitate your budget.

Ⓢ Create a financial diary to track your budget for a month.

Ⓢ Base new budget decisions on areas where your expected expenses and actual expenses don't seem to line up.

Ⓢ Everybody has some waste in their budget, whether it's overpaying for car insurance or spoiled groceries. Find yours to make room for more savings and the items that are important to you and your lifestyle.

Ⓢ Negotiate your rent payment and interest rates on your car loan and credit cards.

Ⓢ Use Internet calculators available on your bank's Web site to compare mortgage and car loans as well as credit cards at different interest rates.

Ⓢ Even seemingly innocent expenses such as groceries can be altered to save money. You may be buying too many high-priced items, allowing groceries to spoil, buying too many items on sale that weren't great deals to begin with, or not using coupons because of time constraints.

Ⓢ Thegrocerygame.com is a great resource for combining coupons with unadvertised and advertised grocery sales.

Ⓢ Use financial budgeting tools such as Manilla to view what's going on in all your accounts, from checking to savings to credit cards, all in one place.

Paying Off Your Non-Student-Loan Debt

Managing your student loans is a huge part of your financial life, but you still have credit card debt, car loans, and possibly a mortgage to deal with. You can improve your overall financial life by finding out all the information you need to know about your non-student-loan debt, organizing your debt, working toward paying off that debt, and evaluating when it's okay to take on new debt. I'll show you how in this chapter.

Ordering Free Credit Reports

Even if you are extremely organized to the point of obsession, a bill slips through the cracks once in awhile. Before you sort through bills and e-bills to find all your credit cards, loan payments, and so on, find out about all your debt by ordering free credit reports from www.annual creditreport.com, a Web site sponsored by the three major credit bureaus: Experian, TransUnion, and Equifax. It offers you one free credit report per year with each of these reporting agencies.

When you get your report, you can find all the information that a creditor would have on you, such as how many times you applied for credit in the past 12 months, your past addresses, collections, and the amounts you owe on all of your credit cards and loans.

For the purpose of gathering a list of your debt, there is no better tool, because it's all right there. You'll also find phone numbers for creditors so you can contact them if you have questions.

You want to get as many of your reports delivered online as possible, because if you create logins with the credit bureaus as you order your reports, you will be able to go online to dispute errors in your report—which will be important if you have any inaccurate information.

> ### Caution
>
> There are many services out there that charge for credit reporting information. Make sure when you type www.annual creditreport.com that you've typed the right address, and don't accidentally click on a service that charges for credit reporting.

Why do you need to look at all three reports? Let's say you look at just one credit report and you use it as a basis for finding all your debt. Oops—one of your student loans isn't listed on your report. You don't notice because you see the seven others from your other semester loans.

How likely is this occurrence? It happened to me when I was looking at my credit reports for the first time. I found collections that were on one report but not on the other two, and I didn't owe the collection. I was able to dispute it and eventually get the collection removed. If I hadn't checked all three reports, I never would have found it and my credit would have been dinged for another five years.

Checklist for Ordering Credit Reports

✓ Go to www.annualcreditreport.com and create a login and order your credit reports every year for free.

✓ Always look at all three reports—from Experian, TransUnion, and Equifax—because you may see information on one report that you don't see on another.

Reviewing Your Entire Debt Portfolio

At this point in the book, you know what you are spending and how your student loans fit into the mix, but now you need to face your credit card, car loan, and total debt package in the same way you faced your student loan debt. Call each creditor or go online to the Web site for your credit account and find your balance information and interest rates.

Your balance information is pretty easy to find, since it will be located near your payment due, but your interest rate is a little different. With car loans, your interest rate was on your initial loan contract at the dealership. But you can also get this information on your statement or by calling your lender. The same goes for any fixed-rate loan, such as a mortgage. The interest you had at day one is generally the interest rate you still have now, unless you refinanced. Even then it's likely to stay at the interest rate you secured during refinancing. Fixed interest rates stay the same over the life of your loan.

Then there are your variable rate loans: personal home equity lines of credit, personal loans, and credit cards. Even if you find your interest rate on your balance statement, it could change. You need to know both the interest rate on these loans and what the rules are for interest rate increases and decreases. You can organize all of this information into a chart in your financial diary or create a computer-generated file.

CREATE A DEBT ORGANIZATION CHART

With the information in your credit reports, along with information you gathered from phone calls, you can create a Debt Organization chart that contains everything you need to know to start to organize and eventually pay off your debt.

For row titles, list all of your loan and credit accounts individually, from your student loans to your credit cards. For columns, use the following category headers:

- Creditor
- Contact phone number
- Interest rate
- Account description, such as Visa ending in 0001
- Payment
- Total due
- Whether your rate can vary
- The term by which your interest rate can vary

With this information, you will know what you have, and that's the first step in developing a credit card payoff strategy. When you review your debt, make sure you don't include payments for items that you know you didn't charge or that should have been marked paid if you pulled them directly from your credit report. You'll deal with these issues separately in the next section.

CREATE A DISPUTED INFORMATION CHART

Create a Disputed Information chart for any disputes you have so all of the information is in one place. Misreported negative information impacts your credit score, and it's not just accounts that shouldn't be on there at all. You should also scan your credit report for reported late payments that you actually made on time. These can impact your credit report and should be disputed.

For this chart, also use your account titles for the rows, such as Visa credit card, account number 123456789000055. (Account numbers are important in this chart because you will need them to file disputes if necessary.) For the columns, use the following categories:

- Creditor
- Collection agency
- Date of the last reported payment
- Date account opened
- Reason why you are disputing the account or payment (this could be because of a duplicate item, a late payment that was actually made on time, or an electric bill for an apartment you lived in for two days that was charged for two months on your report)

When you complete your Disputed Information chart, you can dispute items directly on the Web sites for the three credit bureaus or write a letter. Everything you need to dispute your inaccurate information electronically or in writing is right there in your chart. Handwritten or typewritten letters should be sent to every credit reporting agency reporting the collection, just as you should file your dispute electronically.

Larger Education Equals Smaller Car

When you have a $40,000 student loan, you already have a loan larger than most car loans. So, should you keep driving your old car until the wheels fall off or the engine goes kaput? Not necessarily.

Student loans or not, you still have to get to work and other places. And reliable transportation is key to your life, whether it's a car, public transportation, or a bicycle.

If you need a car where you live, think about the state of your current car and your budget. Is your current car running well? Is a new car really necessary? If your current car is breaking down to the point where a new car would be cheaper, or if you just want to trade it in, evaluate new car payments in terms of your overall budget.

In addition to figuring out how your car payment will fit into your overall budget, think about how it will affect your debt-to-income ratio if you want to qualify for a mortgage or other personal loan. For example, let's say you currently have a debt-to-income ratio (the sum total of your debt payments divided by your income) of over 20 percent. If you bought a car with a $400 monthly payment, you might have a hard time qualifying for a mortgage.

> ### Caution
>
> Don't apply for a car loan until you know you are going to buy a car in the near future. Why? If you are shopping around for a car for a limited time period, your credit is only hit once. However, if you wait weeks or months to make your purchase, every time you apply for new credit, it could drop your score by a few points for a short time period.

You can figure out what your payment might be by using car loan calculators on your bank's Web site and the Web sites of the car dealers where you're considering purchasing your car. On the dealer's Web sites, build and price the car as you would order it and then subtract current rebate offers. This will give you a good estimate of the amount to put in on your bank's Web site to check payments.

If you want to check possible interest rates without filling out an application, check your credit score at myfico.com. You won't ding your credit because you are checking it yourself instead of a potential creditor checking your score, and myfico.com gives estimates of interest rates charged based on credit scores.

If you can wait to buy a vehicle, pay off some of your credit cards first. If you have to use your credit cards to pay your basic bills now, it's not the time to buy a new car—unless it's because of high car repair bills. In that case, buy the cheapest, most reliable used car you can find. Your credit card and student loan payments will thank you, along with your future home.

Checklist for Car Buying When You Have Student Loans

✓ Keep your current car if it is still in good shape.

✓ Use online car loan calculators from your bank to determine car payments.

✓ Car payments can affect your debt-to-income ratio if you want to qualify for a mortgage or other personal loan. Only buy a new car when you truly need one.

✓ Consider the effect of a car payment on your entire budget instead of just what the actual monthly payment will be.

Your First College Credit Cards

Remember when you walked on campus for the first time and right in front of the student union were booths of perky people offering you free t-shirts, pens, and foam soft drink/beer holders? And all you had to do was sign a piece of paper to get your first credit card? So on top of getting free stuff, you were given free money—just like that nice little refund you received from the remainder of your student loan payment.

Those loans may still be haunting you in the form of remaining payments with high interest rates or a charge-off on your credit report. A charge-off is when your credit cards are written off by your credit card company as bad debt. Your card is no longer usable, but the charge-off takes up space on your credit report and reduces your credit score for seven years after your account initially started to fall behind in payments. The credit card company may also still try to collect on this debt.

Unfortunately for most of us, those easy-to-get credit card offers didn't end in college. Except now instead of foam drink holders, we get suckered into getting new credit cards based on the promise of airline miles, travel rewards, shopping sprees at our favorite stores, cash back, or the allure of nifty titles like platinum or black credit cards.

ENDING YOUR RELIANCE ON CREDIT CARDS

In order to pay off your credit cards, you have to stop relying on them. Take the following quick quiz:

1. When you can't afford to pay cash for something, do you put it on your credit card? ____ yes ____ no

2. Do you pay for what you can and then use your credit card to take care of the rest? ____ yes ____ no

3. Do you think if you can afford your monthly minimum payments, it's okay to continue spending? ____ yes ____ no

4. Do you feel like you always have some credit card debt? ____ yes ____ no

5. Do you feel you'll eventually make more money, so it's okay to use a credit card to buy things now? ____ yes ____ no

If you answered "yes" to any of these questions, go back to Chapter 5, "Budgeting for Your Lifestyle and Your Loans," and review the budgeting tips given there. What expenses are keeping you relying on credit cards to pay your monthly bills? What can you cut? You'll never get out of debt as long as you need your credit cards to buy groceries. But once you've got your budget under control, you can move on to the next stage of your life.

Checklist for Ending Credit Card Dependence

✓ Know your credit habits. Do you spend to earn rewards and then lose any gains in finance charges?

✓ Review your budget and make changes if you currently need credit cards just to cover your monthly expenses.

✓ Get rid of any preconceived notions that you have to be in debt forever or that your monthly payment is a part of your life. It is for now, but if you beef up your payments and adjust your budget, it doesn't have to be in the future.

MAKE SURE YOUR PAYMENTS ARE ALWAYS COUNTED ON TIME

The first step to becoming financially stable and responsible is to pay all of your bills on time, every time. This is important for two reasons: Each late payment can ding your credit scores and credit reports for the next seven years, and late fees make it even harder to get out of credit card debt.

Here are just a few ways to ensure that your payments are on time:

- Sign up for online bill pay and statements.
- Sign up to view your accounts online through each individual company.
- Always pay your bills a week before they are due (or pay them the day you receive them).
- Check by phone to make sure your payments arrive.

MAKING MINIMUM PAYMENTS

When your credit card company sends you a statement and tells you what payment is due, that's the minimum payment. The minimum payment is not intended to help you pay off your card, but is simply the minimum amount your credit card will accept every month. This is because your credit card is a line of credit, not a loan.

Making only the minimum payment is dangerous, because unless you make the commitment to make payments as if it were a loan instead of an eternal payment—especially if you keep charging while making minimum payments—you'll be paying off the same $1,000 or $2,000 for up to 20 years!

Always make more than the minimum payments. Even if you only have $500 of credit card debt, if you made minimum payments, it could take you years to pay off your debt. However, if you added just $5 per month to your payments, you could pay off your debt in half the time.

Let's look at an example of how minimum payments on credit cards work. The minimum payment on your credit cards is between 3 and 4 percent of your balance. As your balance goes down, your payment goes down. For instance, if you start off with a $2,000 balance, you don't make additional charges, and your credit card calculates its minimum payment based on 4 percent of your principal (the amount you still have to pay off) and charges 12 percent interest, the chart on the next page shows how much your minimum payment would be for your first six months of payments.

What if you can only afford to make minimum payments? If you decide on a consistent minimum payment that you will make—and don't reduce it as the minimum payment adjusts when the balance is lower—you will pay off your credit card quicker than if you pay the adjusted minimum payments your credit card company gives you.

Payment Number	Payment	Principal Paid	Principal Paid with Static Payment of $80
1	$80	$60	$60
2	$77.60	$58.20	$60.60
3	$75.27	$55.65	$61.21
4	$73.01	$54.76	$61.82
5	$70.82	$53.11	$62.44
6	$68.70	$51.53	$63.06
Total		$333.25	$369.13

Checklist for Making More Than the Minimum Payment

✓ Set up your bill pay for your current minimum payment and don't charge any more on your card until it is paid off. You'll pay off your credit card possibly decades earlier than if you paid off your credit card based on what your credit company adjusts the minimum to each month.

✓ Add $5 or more to your minimum payment when you can. Every dollar helps you pay off your debt that much faster.

✓ Don't look at your credit card bill as a bill you must have forever. However, if you make only the minimum payment and keep using the card, you could have your debt for life.

DOING THE CREDIT CARD SHUFFLE

You're forehead-deep in credit card debt, and every offer you get in the mail for a low-interest balance transfer seems like a great idea. But will a balance transfer help you get rid of your debt forever, or just tuck it away in another credit card?

Let's say you get an offer in the mail for a 0 percent transfer offer for 12 months on new balances. You start juggling in your mind which balance you could transfer that would get you the biggest bang for your buck.

It's not necessarily a bad idea, but here's what you need to think about:

• The balance transfer fee, which can be as much as 5 percent of the amount you're transferring, can cancel out the benefit. For example, if you transfer $5,000 dollars to the new card, you would end up getting charged a fee of $250. What does that equal in 12 percent interest? About five months' worth. Plus, in order to not pay interest, you'd have to pay it off in a year, which would equal a payment of $416.67. You only have $500 a month to make your payments. Thus, you would not even be able to pay your minimum payments on your other cards. As far as fees, you need either a maximum fee of around $100 or less to make the transfer worth it.

- Your other interest rates may still rise. If you use a large percentage of the credit on any card, you could see an interest rate increase on your other cards. If these other cards total $15,000 worth of debt, the interest rate effect could be staggering. Effective July 2010, banks can't raise the rates on your balances you've already charged—but they can darn well raise your rates on future purchases. However, you do want to keep an eye on the news for future credit card legislation.

- You can at least temporarily hurt your credit score and drive up interest rates on future purchases if the balance transfer puts you dangerously close to your credit limit.

- It won't help if you continue to increase your credit card debt level.

While there may not seem like there's much of a case for a 0 percent balance transfer at this point, there are circumstances where you should consider it. If you just want to transfer $1,000 that you will pay off within a year, there isn't a balance transfer fee, and you can still afford to make at least minimum payments on your other cards, it might be a good option.

Consider the following alternatives to a balance transfer:

- Lower your interest rate permanently by negotiating a rate with your bank based on your good customer record and lower rates on your other cards (see Chapter 5).

- Use rewards toward paying off credit card debt.

- Suspend your student loan payments through forbearance or deferment for six months to get rid of part of your credit card debt (preferably eliminate at least one credit card).

MEET YOUR NEW BEST FRIEND: WWW.THOMAS.GOV

You've heard on the news that there's a new credit card bill for consumers that could help you, or more regulations regarding student loans and repayment. Every news source seems to report the details a little bit differently, and you don't know what you qualify for and if the bill applies to you.

The good news is you don't have to rely on any news source; you can go directly to www.thomas.gov. This is my favorite Web site because I can search for and scan any congressional bill for information on new student loan repayment guidelines or tax incentives that are helpful to both me and you. You can search by congressional bill topic, what's on the congressional floor today, or for specific bills you've heard about on the news.

The best way to search is by description. For instance, you can type "student loans" into the search box and find all relevant bills regarding student loans. When you click on a bill, you can search the bill's text to find exactly what you need. And better yet, it tells you whether a bill has passed the House, Senate, or is already signed by the president.

I searched the massive stimulus bill in early 2009 to find out if I qualify for the first-time homebuyer's credit. I couldn't get a complete answer from political offices or the articles I read, but my buddy Thomas helped me. I saw the exact wording and it took me all of 10 minutes versus a couple of hours of pointless phone calls and reading.

Checklist for Searching www.thomas.gov

- ✓ Search www.thomas.gov to verify anything you hear on the news that is important to you.

- ✓ Search by keyword to find the bill you want. Then search through the actual text to find the information you need.

- ✓ Always check the status of the bill. Until it is signed by the president, it's not an official law.

Chapter Wrap-Up

- Order free credit reports on www.annualcreditreport.com. Don't forget to get a credit report from each of the three major bureaus: Experian, TransUnion, and Equifax.

- Create one chart with all your credit card information listed.

- Create a separate chart for information you intend to dispute.

- Buy a car based on what you can afford instead of what you think you deserve. Keep driving your current car if you can, and work on paying down your debt load.

- The first step toward credit freedom is to not live off your credit cards.

- Always strive to pay more than the minimum payment on your credit card balances.

- The two easiest ways to pay off your credit cards faster is to add $5 or more per month to your minimum payment and to set your current minimum payment as a permanent minimum payment until your debt is paid off.

- You will never pay off your debt if you continue to charge items that you don't pay off the same month.

- Keep cards on which you are getting great rewards, that have no annual fees, and that have low interest rates. Do not get a credit card because of sign-on freebies like plane tickets, money, or a television set.

- Make paying on time a high priority. Every late payment is a ding on your credit report and an excuse for credit card companies to raise your interest rates—and you'll get slapped with a late fee to boot.

- When you are thinking about transferring part or all of a balance on one card to another, factor in transfer fees and what the interest rate will be when the balance transfer special interest rate time period ends.

- Whenever you hear about a new program on the news for credit card payments, student loans, or anything else that you are interested in, search for the actual bill on www.thomas.gov.

Understanding How Your Debt Looks to Lenders

You have tons of student loan debt, so why would anyone want to loan you more money or give you a great credit rating that signals to your auto insurance company a heads-up that you deserve the best rates they have to offer? Because you know how to manage your student loans and other debt, and it shows in the two measures lenders use most: your credit scores and your debt-to-income ratio.

Your credit scores reflect how you handle the debt you have, while your debt-to-income ratio reflects how much of your income goes toward your debt payments. If you master how to get the best credit scores and lowest possible debt-to-income ratio, you'll have much less trouble getting home and car loans.

FICO Credit Scores

How do you get the interest rate of your dreams on a car or mortgage loan while you're still carrying around $40,000 plus in student debt? Improve your FICO credit score.

FICO scores determine what interest rate readers will have for up to 30 years. It could make hundreds of dollars of difference in your monthly payments—equivalent to a student loan payment off your mortgage.

WHAT FACTORS GO INTO CALCULATING YOUR CREDIT SCORE?

FICO scores, the most common form of credit scoring, uses a system of scoring based on how you utilize your credit, the length of your credit history, how often you apply for credit, and any credit delinquencies. The following information is based on information provided by FICO on www.fico.com.

Payment History: 35 Percent

This portion of your score reflects how you've handled your credit thus far. It includes whether you've paid your loans and credit cards on time; whether you've had a public record in the financial arena, such as a bankruptcy or lien on your home due to nonpayment of a work order; how many collections and past-due accounts you've had in the last seven years; how late you were or still are on a payment; how long it's been since you've been late on a payment; and how many accounts are currently paid on time.

> **Caution**
>
> Bankruptcies stay on your credit reports and factor into your credit scores for ten years, and a collection can stay on your reports and affect your score for seven years. However, the further you get from any negative occurrence on your credit reports, the less it affects your score.

Currently paid on time refers to your most recent payments. If you have a late payment on an account from six months ago, but you are currently paying on time, the past-due payment will still count against you. However, the longer you are able to pay your bills on time, the less the past late payment will matter.

Amount Owed: Approximately 30 Percent

This is the second-largest part of your credit score and the easiest to fix because all you have to do is reduce your credit balances. You don't have to worry about how your payments were made in the past; you just need to have a plan to reduce your card and loan balances in the future.

Let's say you have two open cards. One has a credit limit of $2,000 and you owe $1,500. The other has a limit of $500 and you owe $100. On the first card, you're using 75 percent of your available credit. On the second card, you're using 20 percent of your credit. For your total available balance you are using 53 percent of your available credit. Your credit score considers both the 53 percent and the individual card credit usage of 75 percent and 20 percent. What this means is that it's best to pay off your smaller balance first. Doing so will decrease your overall credit utilization, plus you drop your credit utilization on this card from 20 percent to 0 percent with only a $100 payment. To drop your other card by 20 percent of the available balance would take a $400 payment.

Ideally, you want to keep your credit cards under 15 percent usage individually and as a group to optimize this part of your credit score. It doesn't matter whether you've had these cards for ten years or ten months—only that you keep your balances low. While other factors do play some role in this part of your score, pay the most attention to your revolving accounts (credit card balances).

Length of Credit History: 15 Percent

Your length of credit history is the part of your credit score that reflects how long you've had credit. It factors in when you opened both your oldest credit cards and your newest credit cards.

While logic says the highest scores are awarded to people who have the oldest credit cards, there is a trick to this that you need to be aware of: Each new card factors into your average. For example, let's say you've had a credit card for 15 years, so you think you're doing great in the credit history department. However, a couple of years ago, you got caught up in the 0 percent credit offer craze when you were furnishing your new home and signed up for two new credit cards and a retail account. Now your average credit history is around five years.

On the low-credit history side, let's say you just got your first card in years three years ago, and now your credit's getting better and you get two new cards. You now have an average credit history average of one year.

Types of Credit Used: 10 Percent

To get the best score in this portion of your credit score, you should have a mix of installment loans, credit cards, and store cards. However, it's not going to make enough of a difference if you don't have a retail credit card to justify going out and getting one. You could end up getting yourself into debt further by adding an extra card, and the one card type won't make a huge difference in your credit score.

New Credit: 10 Percent

This part of your score is about how you are using new credit. How many times you've applied for credit, whether you've rebounded from past credit problems by being responsible with your credit now, and how many of your accounts were opened recently are all considered.

The goal in this section is two-fold: to not apply for credit too often and to show responsibility with the credit you have. If you are just getting back into the credit game you need a credit card to reestablish positive credit history, but it's not a good idea to get a gas card, a retail card, and bank

> ## Caution
>
> If you already have credit cards with established payment history, do not open new cards for the sake of building new credit. It will not raise your FICO score.

card all within the same month. Think about why you are getting a new card, and give yourself a few months to a year between opening new cards, especially if you are rebuilding credit.

Checklist for Understanding the Components of FICO Scoring

- ✓ Thirty percent of your score is based solely on how close you are to maxing out your credit cards. Using your credit cards less frequently is one of the easiest ways to increase your score.

- ✓ Limit how often you apply for new credit. Whether the credit you have is six months old or thirty years old, a new card will decrease your credit history and increase your new credit applications.

- ✓ While you can't change a late payment history, every month that you pay your credit cards on time is one more month of on-time credit reporting.

Debunking Urban Credit Score Myths

FICO scoring expert Barry Paperno tells you everything you need to know to achieve a great credit score.

Myth: The amount of your student loan debt will negatively impact your FICO score.

Fact: Don't worry about whether the amount of your student debt is $60,000 or $300,000—or even the interest rate—when it comes to your credit score. What you have to worry about most is paying on time.

Myth: Student loan debt is scored the same way as credit card debt.

Fact: Student loan debt is not treated the same in regards to your credit score as credit card debt. It's an installment loan. There are two major kinds of debt: revolving debt and installment debt. The amount you owe on an installment loan is relatively unimportant to your score. Other types of installment loans include mortgages and car loans. However, with revolving debt such as credit cards, it is important to keep your balances low compared to your credit limits. For example, it's never a good idea to max out your credit cards.

Myth: Once you are married, your credit score combines with your spouse's score.

Fact: You still have individual scores, whether you've been married 65 years or you were married yesterday. However, you will have credit history in common every time you add your spouse's name to one of your credit cards as either an authorized user or joint account holder. An authorized user is authorized to sign for charges on your credit cards but is not responsible for paying the debt, while a joint account holder is equally responsible for all charges. Either way that you add your spouse to an account, the payment history on the new user's credit report will extend all the way back to the original date of the credit card's opening. Make sure that whenever a name is added to an account that it doesn't hurt the credit rating of the person being added, meaning the account doesn't have late pays and has a low rate of credit utilization. After all, you don't want to add your spouse to a credit card that is maxed out until you have paid down the balance.

Myth: You should marry someone with good credit.

Fact: It's a good idea for both of you to share credit reports and credit scores with each other prior to getting married, so you know from which point you are starting. But one's credit history shouldn't necessarily make or break a marriage decision, as past mistakes and misfortunes are often learning opportunities. One of you could have recovered from high credit card debt in the past, but the other could have recovered from bankruptcy. What is important is that no matter what your experiences were in the past, you come together with a plan to improve both of your scores and stop the habits that created them. While your scores won't unite in marriage, your financial lives will likely merge for major purchases such as buying a home.

Myth: When you change your name, your credit is affected.

Fact: Your credit moves with your name.

Myth: Consolidating your student loans will increase or decrease your credit score.

Fact: Your decision to consolidate won't have much of an impact. The decision to consolidate or not consolidate should be based on whether you want your loan extended or whether you want your loans streamlined to one loan payment.

Myth: The more credit cards you have, the better your score you will be.

Fact: All you need to achieve a good credit score is one credit account open longer than six months. Especially if you are in credit-rebuilding mode, do not open too many new credit cards.

Myth: Too much credit available is considered risky by lenders.

Fact: We don't find that. In fact, it's better to keep an unused charge card open than to close the account, because part of your score depends on how low your combined credit utilization rate is among all your credit cards. But you still may want to close an unused account with an annual fee, as long as it is not your only credit card.

Myth: What is once a good score is always a good score.

Fact: Credit markets can loosen or tighten over time. While a score of 670 may earn you a great interest rate one year, it may not in the following year. Check www.myfico.com for average interest rates for mortgage and car loans based on credit score ranges to get an idea of the interest rates you can expect with your credit score.

Bottom line: To build the best credit score possible, pay your bills on time while maintaining low credit card balances, and open new accounts only when needed. Your score will continue to improve as long as you maintain these good credit habits.

LOW CREDIT SCORES HAPPEN

Maybe you have credit card debt from college that you are still paying off, or you've been so busy trying to figure out how to pay your loans that you missed a credit card payment and your credit score dropped by a few points. Now it's going to take seven years for that one missed payment to no longer show up on your credit report.

Low credit scores can happen in numerous ways, but they can be exponentially raised in a short period of time. How? In short, by making all your debt payments on time, not shying away from credit accounts completely, and managing your current credit accounts well.

Here are the easiest ways to improve a credit score:

- **If you still have a credit card, keep your balance as low as possible.** However, you don't want to leave the card unused. You can't build better credit unless you make at least a minor charge each month. But you can pay it off that month to avoid interest charges.

- **Get a new card if you don't have one.** You can't make up for past credit indiscretions unless there is something positive to counteract it. Apply for credit cards that allow for little or no credit history. You can find these online. Don't be afraid of annual fees. If you can only qualify for a card with a small annual fee, it's worth it to rebuild your credit.

- **Pay on time, every time.** From your student loan on down, the best thing you can do for your credit is to make all your payments on time.

- **Dispute inaccurate information on your credit report.** Knocking off a collection that doesn't belong can instantly increase your credit score. (I'll discuss disputing information on your credit report a little later in this chapter.)

Caution

There is a difference between a card with an annual fee and one with an application fee. The latter type of card can end up eating away half a small credit limit in fees and should be avoided. If you can get approved for an unsecured credit card with an application fee, consider a secured credit card. With a secured credit card, you have offer money in a separate bank account to secure the amount of the credit limit. You apply for a secured card in the same way you would apply for an unsecured card, but the approval process is much easier because of the deposit provided. You will get the money back that you secured your card with after a specified period of time and number of consistent on-time payments.

What Different Scores Mean

What your credit score means varies depending on how others are maintaining their credit. It's kind of like the SATs, where you are judged based on your habits on a percentile basis. For instance, 620 was once considered a good score that would keep you in the running for any mortgage, but when the credit market is tight, a higher score of 700 may be needed. The scoring system didn't change. A 620 was earned in the same way it was earned when credit was given out more freely, and the 700 was earned in the same way as when credit was given out more conservatively.

So how do you get a score that will get you the best rates in any economic conditions? The same way you worked to get the best SAT score: Study hard, know the material, check your answers, and hope for the best.

Here are two basic rules everyone needs to follow to maintain or improve their credit score:

- **Avoid applying for more than one or two credit lines at a time.** One of the components of your credit score is how often you apply for credit. If you apply for eight credit cards in a year, lenders are going to be wary of why you need so many new cards at once.

- **Don't buy a new car right before you want to buy a new home.** Every time you apply for credit, it's a ding on your credit score. Plus, the car loan will increase your debt-to-income ratio.

For a good indicator of what your score means in the current economy, go to www.myfico.com and click on "credit" to find the chart where mortgage and car loans are categorized by credit score. This chart is updated regularly and will provide you a great idea of what you can expect if you have to get a loan with your current score.

Disputing Mistakes on Your Credit Reports

When you look at your credit reports from all three credit bureaus (Experian, TransUnion, and Equifax), you notice a collection on an electric bill for an apartment you never lived in. Your credit score is based on information contained on your credit report, and if you have inaccurate negative information on your credit report for debt that began as more than $100, it could decrease your credit score by a few points or more—depending on how recent the debt is—for no reason.

If there's a mistake on your credit report, you can get it corrected. Experian, TransUnion, and Equifax all have online dispute forms for correcting your credit. Since each credit bureau may have slightly different information, only send dispute forms to the ones with the inaccurate information reported. (See Chapter 4, "Managing Your Private Loans and Payoff Strategies," for more on reviewing your credit reports.)

All the information you need to file a dispute is in your Disputed Information chart, which you created in Chapter 6, "Paying Off Your Non-Student-Loan Debt."

You may also find out about a collection on an item you forgot about or that didn't occur by receiving a letter in the mail or getting denied for a car loan, mortgage, or credit card. Respond within 30 days of being notified. The faster you respond, the better your chances of avoiding a collection agency or a bill collector reporting the debt to the credit bureaus at all. Any collection agency or debt holder is required to show proof within 30 days that you actually owe the bill if you ask for the bill to be provided.

When it comes to debt, your creditor has the burden of proof. So if you dispute a credit reporting error on your report, it is the creditor's burden to provide the bill that shows you still owe the amount. If they are able to provide a bill, then you may have to show proof that you did pay the bill. You can prove a payment was made by digging up old bank or credit card statements

Checklist for Disputing Credit Report Mistakes

✓ Review your credit report and highlight anything that could be a mistake.

✓ Dispute the mistake using an online dispute form, when possible.

✓ If you send a dispute letter, give the reasons why you feel it was a mistake, such as duplicate information, the bill was already paid, or you never owed the amount listed.

✓ Gather supporting materials. Order bank account statements for credit cards and bank accounts.

Bad Credit Cards Build Good Credit

If you've had credit card trouble in the past, you probably would rather never look at a credit card again—especially when you think of another payment on top of the payments you are already making to student loans, car loans, rent, or a mortgage. You can't fix your previous bad credit without showing you can handle credit now. But how do you get a credit card when your credit isn't up to snuff?

Look for credit cards that are specifically directed toward those without an excellent credit rating or get a secured credit card. With these kinds of cards, you can expect annual fees and low limits. The annual fee is worth it. When two years from now your insurance rates are lower and you can get a home or a car at a much lower interest rate than you can now, you'll be happy you paid $20 to $50 for an annual fee. The goal should be to find the lowest annual fee out there. Consider at least three different options, and be wary of high application fees. (I've had offers sent to me with fees totaling over $100 on a $300 limit!)

Reporting to all three major bureaus is as vital to choosing a credit card as the amount of the annual fee. A credit card with no annual fee wouldn't be worth it if the credit card company doesn't report your credit history to all three bureaus. Before you sign your name to any contract or application, verify how credit reporting is conducted.

Once you get your card, treat your credit limit the same way you would a larger limit—with extreme caution. You want your usage to reflect fiscal responsibility, so limit your monthly spending to 15 percent of your credit line. Use the following chart as an easy reference guide for figuring out what 15 percent of your credit limit is.

Credit Limit	15 Percent
$500	$75
$1,000	$150
$2,000	$300
$4,000	$600
$10,000	$1,500

If you don't want to think about charging something that is below 15 percent of your credit limit each month, try a recurring payment that is the exact same every month such as gym memberships, online movie rental memberships or your grocerygame.com membership. When you put one of these recurring payments on your card, also add a recurring payment to your bank account to cover the charge each month. That way you can almost forget about it. However, you should double-check that your payment is credited before the due date.

Before you apply for a credit card for those without excellent credit or get a secured credit card, make sure you actually need to do so. Check your credit scores—you may have better credit than you thought.

Checklist for What to Look for in Credit Cards for Those with Credit Scores Needing Improvement

✓ There are plenty of credit cards out there that will accept individuals with less-than-perfect credit. You will probably have to pay an annual fee, but how much is the key. Compare the fees among at least three cards.

✓ Watch out for high application fees that eat up your credit limit.

✓ Verify the credit card company reports to the three major credit bureaus (Equifax, TransUnion, and Experian) on a monthly basis. If the credit card is not reporting to all three bureaus, you won't get the credit score boost you need.

Debt-to-Income Ratio

Your best friend has managed to buy a house with an incredible interest rate, and she makes $2,000 a year less than you do and has $10,000 more in student loan debt than you do. Yet, when you spoke to a mortgage broker, you were told your interest rate would be 2 percent higher, and only if you bought a much cheaper house than your friend's. To add to the confusion, you checked your credit score, and it's 10 points higher than your friend's.

What gives?

Credit scores, income, and the amount of debt will only help you so much you when you want to get a home loan. You also need to have a low debt-to-income ratio. Your debt-to-income ratio is the ratio of your debt as compared to your income. Your friend could have a smaller debt-to-income ratio because of lower payments on his student loans, or because of extended payments and smaller credit card loan debt.

For example, let's assume the following scenario.

Your friend's situation:

Income: $60,000 per year, which is $5,000 per month

Credit cards: total of $2,000 with minimum payments of 4 percent, totaling $80 per month

Student loan payment on $60,000 consolidated for 30 years at interest of 4.5 percent: $304.01

Car loan: $20,000 for 5 years at 5 percent: $377.42

Total debt payments: $761.43

Debt-to-income ratio before a mortgage: $761.43 ÷ $5,000 = 15.23 percent

Your situation:

Income: $62,000 per year, which is $5,166 per month

Credit cards: total of $4,000 with minimum payments of 4 percent, totaling $160 per month

Student loan payment on $50,000 for 10 years at 4.5 percent: $518.19

Car loan: $20,000 for 5 years at 5 percent: $377.42

Total debt payments: $1,055.61

Debt-to-income ratio before a mortgage: $1,055.61 ÷ $5,166 = 20.43 percent

As you can see, your friend has a debt-to income ratio that is 5 percent less than yours. Since mortgage lenders are generally wary of lending to borrowers with more than 41 percent of their income going to all their debt payments plus their mortgage note, insurance, and property tax, you're in a worse position than your friend is.

Forty-one percent of $5,000 per month income is $2,050, meaning after subtracting $761.43 for debt payments, this person has $1,288.57 left for housing expenses. The person who makes $5,166 per month in this example has a 41 percent debt-to-income ratio at $2,118.33. After subtracting $1,055.61 for other debt payments, this person only has $1,062.72 left for housing expenses. Thus, the first person can qualify for $226 more a month in home payments.

What lessons can you learn from this example?

- The amount of your student loan debt alone does not affect lending situations; it's your payment.
- Consolidating your loans will increase your chances of getting approved for a mortgage because it reduces your monthly debt payments.
- Watch your credit card spending. This will affect getting a mortgage as much as your student loan payment.

To calculate your debt-to-income ratio, add up all of your debt payments: credit cards, student loans, and other debts. For credit cards, use your minimum payments. Divide your total debt number by your pre-tax monthly income. Here's the formula:

> Credit card minimum payments + student loan payments + car loan payments + personal loan payments ÷ pre-tax monthly income = debt-to-income ratio

Once you've calculated your debt-to-income ratio, analyze it for ways you could improve. You can have a low debt-to-income ratio with a large amount of student loan debt. Just organize your student loan payment into a lower monthly payment and watch your overall debt.

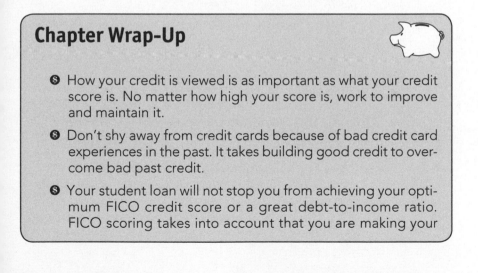

Chapter Wrap-Up

- How your credit is viewed is as important as what your credit score is. No matter how high your score is, work to improve and maintain it.
- Don't shy away from credit cards because of bad credit card experiences in the past. It takes building good credit to overcome bad past credit.
- Your student loan will not stop you from achieving your optimum FICO credit score or a great debt-to-income ratio. FICO scoring takes into account that you are making your

payments on time, while your debt-to-income ratio looks at your monthly payments on all your debt in relation to your monthly income.

- Even if you do pay off your credit cards every month, do not use more than 15 percent of your credit limit at any time.

- Credit cards are about your total debt picture. Think about how your credit card payment could affect your approval for your home loan.

- Know what your debt-to-income ratio is and work to improve it.

Surviving Debt and Relationships

You love your partner with all your heart, but you're not so sure about his or her spending habits. You wonder what credit card debt is behind all the trips you go on or the snazzy clothes you always admire on your partner. On the other hand, you have $40,000 in student loan debt that you may have yet to come clean on. Or your partner is the very definition of perfect credit, who has never missed a payment on anything or misused a credit card.

Debt Meets Relationship

It's time for both you and your partner to come clean by displaying all the bills on the table. You need to know exactly what you are getting yourself into, and so does your partner. This is because the bills that you are bringing into the marriage can multiply well into your marriage if one of you likes to live beyond your means.

Take a deep breath, because you are about to prepare for the bill and credit talk. Here are the steps I suggest for having the "talk":

1. **Stop feeling guilty.** The first step in this chapter is the same as the first step in this book—forgive yourself for your student loans and past spending. As of today, you still have all your debt—student debt and otherwise—but you can no longer punish yourself for it. After all, you don't have a time machine to borrow less and save more. Instead of feeling guilty, have a plan on how you are going to change your habits when you present your full financial

disclosure. Also, if you've been consistent with making payments, mention it. You can counter your debt with how well you've done at making payments. However, if you're currently overdrawn on your bank account or maxed out on your credit cards, explain to your partner why you are in that situation and how you are dedicated to changing your habits.

2. **Prepare for financial intimacy.** Show off your financial know-how by making a plan together. You'd pre-budget car payments for a car you are planning on purchasing. Why not pre-budget your life together? Each one of you should get a copy of your credit reports from the three major bureaus (Experian, TransUnion, and Equifax) so that you're both aware of all your bills. It's also a good idea to get your credit scores from www.myfico.com. This way you can show that although you have high debt, you have actual proof that you can pay your bills on time—if this is the case. If not, you can talk about how you will work together to change your situation.

   If you are marrying Mr. or Ms. Pristine Credit who has never had a student loan or made one late payment—dispel the myth that high student loan debt equals lower chance of mortgage approval. As you learned in Chapter 7, "Understanding How Your Debt Looks to Lenders," this is not the case. Most banks will look at your debt-to-income ratio, which includes only the dollar amount of monthly payments, not your total amount of debt you owe. For instance, if a $20,000 car is on a five-year payment plan, the payment could be higher than one on your $60,000 student loan with a 30-year payment plan. Thus, the $20,000 car would weigh more heavily into a home loan decision than the $60,000 student loan.

3. **Be able to explain how you pay your bills.** It's not necessarily the amount of debt someone brings into a relationship that causes problems, but how committed that person is to repaying it. Whether you are committing to someone for life or considering a long-term commitment, you should ask your partner the following questions:

   • How well do you budget for your expenses?

   • Are you living within your means?

   • Why and how did you accumulate your debt?

4. **Listen to your partner's explanations thoughtfully.** It's just as hard for your partner to talk about his or her debt as it is for you to talk about yours.

5. **Evaluate but don't judge debt.** Whatever someone did in the past is in the past. But it's important to have a solid mindset for the future.

Combining Credit

When I entered a past relationship, my credit was a mess. My bankruptcy was still being processed, and the only credit cards I had were charge-offs. As we grew closer, he was afraid to commit because he thought my credit would prevent us from buying a home. He wanted my credit fixed—before we got more serious. He wasn't being unreasonable in wanting me to fix my credit problems—and the habits that caused them.

You need to know how your partner's spending and credit history will affect you so you can decide what to expect from your partner as far as cleaning up his or her credit mistakes—or helping you correct your own credit or spending habits. Here are some questions to consider:

- **Are your credit reports and scores automatically combined?** No. Credit reports and scores are similar to Social Security numbers. They represent one person and one person only. Your credit history and credit score take into account your individual credit habits since you charged your first purchase back in college or were issued your first student loan. Your credit history may be even older if you were an authorized user on one of your parent's accounts as a child or teenager.

- **How will your partner's spending habits affect your credit?** Let's say you shop at discount department stores and are careful about all of your purchases. Your perspective husband drives a new car every two years and charges freely on his credit cards— although he stays current on all his cards. What does this mean to your credit? Credit, financial responsibility issues, and emotional issues all have different answers. Credit-wise, your partner's debt only affects you if your name is on the account either as a co-signer, joint account holder, or authorized user. Emotionally, you may start to get jealous that he always gets the car, while you still drive the same car you did in college. The payment for the car he drives will come out of your household money. And the debt may affect your mutual ability to save for retirement.

- **Does living together versus being married make a difference on responsibility levels?** Yes. If you are living together, you don't have to worry about technically being responsible for your partner's debt by marital laws. However, when you build your life with someone, you need to be comfortable with how that person handles money.

WHEN ARE YOU RESPONSIBLE FOR SOMEONE ELSE'S DEBT?

When you commit to a potentially life-long relationship with someone, your financial lives are going to intertwine. You can become responsible for your partner's debt in a variety of ways. If you co-sign for a loan, you are both responsible. If you are both on a mortgage note, you are both responsible for the debt.

If you sign on as a joint account holder on each other's credit cards, you are jointly responsible for each other's credit card debt. If you sign on as an authorized user, you can use your partner's credit cards, but you aren't responsible for her debt. The bottom line is that you want to be completely committed to someone and comfortable with each other's spending habits before you become financially intertwined.

> **Caution**
>
> Even if you feel completely comfortable using each other's credit cards, avoid becoming an authorized user or joint account holder on credit cards that have a significantly smaller credit history than yours or have late pays. When you sign on as an authorized user or joint account holder, you are taking along the complete history of that card for duplication on your credit report.

VIEWING EACH OTHER'S CREDIT REPORTS

If you want to get every penny out in the open before you share your pennies, don't just order credit reports for both of you and go over them together. Make a chart. This chart is different from the one you created in Chapter 6, "Paying Off Your Non-Student-Loan Debt," because this is basically an on-paper version of the credit/bill talk. With a chart, you can look at you and your partner's debts and discuss why they happened. Everything is out on the table and in writing.

The rows should be for the name of the loan, credit card, or collection. Columns should include the following:

- **Amount of debt.** This is the total amount owed on each of your accounts. Total these amounts for each person on the bottom on the chart.

- **Interest rate.** Noting the interest rate will help you figure out how long it will take to pay off the loan.

- **Payment.** Note whether this is the minimum payment that is required, or a larger amount you determined in order to pay off your debt faster.

- **How you plan to pay it off.** Do you or your partner plan on using workplace bonuses or tax refunds to pay off the debt faster? Are you budgeting extra money toward paying off the debt? For installment loans (such as student loans and car loans that are for a fixed amount and have a fixed payment every month), do you plan on making only the payments that will pay it off on time instead of early?

- **Why the debt happened.** If your partner has a lot of credit card debt, you want to know why and if he is still charging items to supplement his lifestyle. This is the category that will lead to the most discussion on how you can fix this problem together.

There isn't a definitive answer on how much debt is acceptable, but each partner must take the necessary steps to fix past debt problems.

HOW SEPARATE ACCOUNTS CAN CAUSE TURMOIL

You disagree on how to spend your fun money and you're used to spending money on whatever you want, when you want. So you decide to have separate accounts. After all, why mix money and love?

Meanwhile, you pool your money to pay bills, but your credit card bills are separate and perhaps even unknown to your significant other. Five years later, your partner has $20,000 in credit card debt—buying clothing; expensive presents for you, his family, and his friends; and weekend getaways with you or his buddies—while you have $20,000 in a savings account.

Your partner loses his job and can no longer pay his credit card debts on time. You married your honey for better or for worse, so the $20,000 you've saved is now going toward paying your partner's credit card debt. On top of your money going toward that debt, your partner tells you in order to look the part when interviewing for new jobs, he has to have new clothes, and he will keep buying his family presents so no one suspects anything's wrong.

Agreeing to separate accounts once you are married will not solve fundamental problems and differences when it comes to your money attitudes. In fact, it's the easiest way for you to get into money trouble faster, because the less-frugal spouse can spend money without the other spouse knowing, and that will keep him from helping to save for a child's college education, saving for what should be your mutual retirement, or contributing to an emergency fund.

Have the talk about money—even after your trip down the aisle—and always include what your financial future looks like as well as your individual financial pasts. If you still want separate play money, set aside a certain amount for play. It can even be in a separate checking or savings account. But don't let the separate play money be on credit cards—and especially don't let it be on new credit cards that one of you doesn't know about. The marriages with the most trust and fewest fights over money are the ones where everything is out in the open and money differences can be solved as a team. Just because your honey has bad credit doesn't mean he always will. You can help your partner develop better habits by your example and by discussing and planning budgets together. Commit to a common goal of good credit and staying on budget for both of you.

Checklist for Having Separate Bank Accounts

✓ Don't get separate bank accounts to avoid communication over finances.

✓ Even if you keep separate credit cards from before you were married, show each other the bills regularly.

✓ If you are going to have any kind of separate account, let it be a fun account for your monthly play money.

Saying "I Do" on a Budget

Weddings are wonderful occasions that don't need to be overshadowed by adding $20,000 to $40,000 to your debt. Follow some of these tips from Robbi Ernst III, president and founder of June Wedding, Inc., and author of *Great Wedding Tips from the Experts: What Every Bride Can Learn from the Most Successful Wedding Planners*, for an amazing wedding that won't bust your budget. (Go to the June Wedding, Inc. Web site at www. junewedding.com for more tips.)

- If your budget is tight, think beyond ballrooms when choosing a location for your reception. A family home that's already decorated for the holidays can be a beautiful location, your apartment community center could have an area that is rented to residents for a few hundred dollars or less, or you could have it in the park or restaurant where you took a stroll or had dinner on your first date.

- Hire a competent college student or enlist a friend or family member to take pictures.

- If you have a friend who's handy in the kitchen, ask her to bake the wedding cake.

- Make your own invitations. Check your local arts and crafts stores for invitation kits and make it a project the two of you can share.

- Cut down your wedding list.

- Flowers and food are where people usually go over budget, so be extra cautious in these areas.

- Hire a professionally certified wedding consultant for help in finding vendors and venues within your budget. Doing so will actually save you money. Talk about what the consultant charges for the appointment ahead of time.

- Have a simple cocktail party reception with two or three hors d'oeuvres instead of a sit-down dinner.

- Don't charge anything on a credit card. Stick to the budget that you, your partner, and your families agreed upon.

- Have your wedding on a weekday, which can be much cheaper for venues than a weekend.

The One-Income Household

When both of you make good incomes, getting together as a couple seems like a way to have an even more fabulous life. But hold your dream vacations and fantasy car-buying purchase until you've thought about what happens if one of you gets laid off or decides to stay home to raise a child. You may be stuck with one income, but are you prepared to manage on one salary?

Here are some questions to contemplate and discuss with your partner if you are already married:

- Could you get by on one income if necessary?
- How much of both incomes do you use now?
- How is your fun money handled? Are both you and your partner aware of where most, if not all, of your income is going?
- Does one spouse have ambitions of staying home with children?
- Do your jobs feel stable?
- Do you put away large amounts of savings each month?

If you are thinking about getting married, here are some questions to ask:

- Is each paycheck exhausted by the end of the month?
- What will be the budgetary differences when you share one home and expenses such as car insurance?

Try this exercise with your partner. Write lists separately of what each of you would like to buy in the next five years. Then search the Internet for current prices. For example, you might list the following:

- Television
- Electronics
- Jewelry
- Your first home
- A new car
- Vacations

Compare your lists and discuss how these items fit into your overall budget, then construct a budget that only uses one person's income to pay all of your combined bills. See Chapter 5, "Budgeting for Your Lifestyle and Your Loans," for examples. Make sure you've included personal must-haves for both of you in the budget.

The trick is you want to do this exercise separately first, and then create a budget together. This will give you insight into how your partner looks at money. For example, did she estimate a grocery budget that would barely feed a squirrel? You want to find out why and if it's a point you'll need to iron out. Is it because she lives on the cheapest items she can buy, or because she's a savvy coupon-clipper?

After you've completed the second stage of this budgeting exercise and developed a sample budget, ask yourselves if you would be able to live on one income. If your basic expenses wouldn't be covered, review Chapter 5 to reevaluate your expenses. If you worked toward paying off your credit cards together, would a one-income situation be more manageable? Would you be able to survive on one income after your credit cards are paid off? Is there another expense you could cut in case you had to live on one income? Are your car payments about to end, and you plan on keeping your car another two or three years?

You may never have to live on one income, but being able to is one way of working toward a more secure financial future.

Checklist for Living on One Income

✓ Construct budgets for what you currently spend as individuals.

✓ Include must-have personal items in each of your lists.

✓ Keep an open mind about the other person's spending. There may be items that you spend money on that would never make sense to your partner, such as a car or computer hobby, yoga, or decorating. Categorize these items as pleasure activities that deserve equal budgetary consideration.

✓ If you could survive on one income if you didn't have credit card or car loan debt, start using the income of the person who makes less money solely to pay off credit card and car loan debts. Make sure you don't regrow the credit card debt. Buy your next car based on the payments you could afford if one of you no longer worked.

Case Study: A Life in Student Loans

When Dawn received her first student loan bill six months after graduation—amounting to half her salary—her financial life flashed before her eyes. With over $50,000 in federal student loan debt, she rethought every expenditure she had made during college and whether it had been the best move for her financial future: going out (clubs, dinners, drinking, gas money, gifts for friends), clothes, and stuff for her apartment. Was it all necessary, and what was it worth to her now? If she had just refused some of her aid money and forgone a few of these expenses, would she still have this gargantuan bill sitting in front of her? Would she have charged what she couldn't pay for with student loan refund checks on her credit cards?

"So many of the things I put on my credit cards at that time, I have given away, donated to charity, no longer own because I outgrew them, or were so temporary to begin with that I should have paid for them with cash or done without," Dawn says.

Did she really need the Capital One credit card with the "Starry Nights" picture on it that she opened in college, which she picked solely because of the image of Van Gogh's painting instead of the terms of the credit card or the interest rates?

"For the first and last time, I charged too close to my limit, received a late fee, went over my limit, was charged an over-the-limit fee, and had to struggle to pay it back down to a manageable amount so I would stop incurring fees," says Dawn. "As soon as I was able to, I paid that card off, cut up the card, and closed the account. After that experience, I learned to pay more careful attention to the fine print when accepting a credit card offer."

Dawn acted fast and consolidated her student loans at a rate of under 6 percent for 30 years. But consolidating her student loans didn't mean they wouldn't still take up half her salary. She had to make payments for two months until the company she chose to consolidate with officially controlled all her student loan debt.

She's made mistakes with making late payments on her credit cards, but she survived financially with two strategies: buying a modest home, and paying student loans and the mortgage before anything else. Before she tabulates what she has available for a car or a home, she looks at her student loan debt first.

Her husband, who came into the marriage with no debt, always recognized the importance of her student loans. He took initiative when planning their future and regarded her student loans as one of the first payments they needed to make as couple.

When they bought a house, they decided that the monthly $250 student loan payment should be subtracted from any calculation of what they could afford for a mortgage. The student loan payment is also a factor in determining what car they drive.

Dawn started making extra payments on her student loans to pay them off faster before she had to take a temporary reprieve due to the combined extra responsibility of a new child and taking on more of the family finances when her husband took a pay cut in a tough economy. Her husband helped her by making her student debt a priority, and she repaid the favor by helping with his credit card debt.

Still shy of 30 years old when interviewed, Dawn and her husband had their own home and were about to welcome their first child into their family.

What does Dawn's story teach the rest of us?

- **Establish priorities.** Before you consider any new purchases, consider the payments on what was probably your first major purchase—your education.

- **Know the terms of your credit cards.** I chose a particular credit card because I could add a picture of my dog, but also because it has a great rewards program. It's okay to have a pretty credit card, but you should make sure it also has terms you can live with.

- **Learn from your past spending habits.** Whether, like Dawn, you overspent in college, or you are splurging now, think about each purchase. Will you be happy you made the purchase tomorrow, one year from now, or even five years from now?

Chapter Wrap-Up

- To get copies of both of your FICO credit scores, go to www.myfico.com.
- Both you and your partner have a financial past. It's who you are as a couple, and the lessons you've learned will help you have a successful financial future.

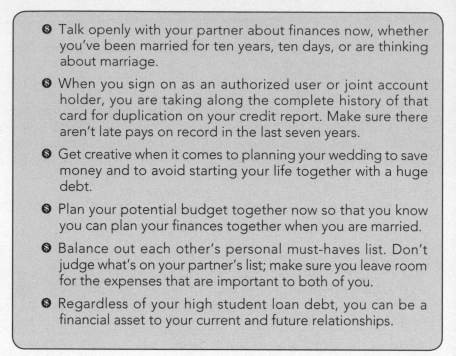

- ⑤ Talk openly with your partner about finances now, whether you've been married for ten years, ten days, or are thinking about marriage.

- ⑤ When you sign on as an authorized user or joint account holder, you are taking along the complete history of that card for duplication on your credit report. Make sure there aren't late pays on record in the last seven years.

- ⑤ Get creative when it comes to planning your wedding to save money and to avoid starting your life together with a huge debt.

- ⑤ Plan your potential budget together now so that you know you can plan your finances together when you are married.

- ⑤ Balance out each other's personal must-haves list. Don't judge what's on your partner's list; make sure you leave room for the expenses that are important to both of you.

- ⑤ Regardless of your high student loan debt, you can be a financial asset to your current and future relationships.

Budgeting During Inflation

When energy bills, food prices, and rent payments rise and you have high student loan debt, how do you keep your budget intact without impacting your lifestyle? Find inexpensive ways to curtail the effects of rising expenses. After all, your student loans are a static expense, even if you postpone your loans due to a temporary financial setback.

In this chapter we'll look at just a few ways you can save buckets of money while only spending tablespoons worth—thus, getting your budget ready to conquer any inflationary situation.

Saving on Your Electricity Bill

You may not have a few thousand dollars to shell out for new energy-efficient windows and doors, or you may be renting a home and not want to put that kind of money into a home you don't own. That's why it's so great that there are simple things you can do to save electricity without spending more than $50.

Try these simple measures to save money on your electric bill:

- Install fluorescent light bulbs. A 15-watt fluorescent bulb uses a quarter of the electricity that a 60-watt incandescent light bulb does. And since they last longer, you'll recoup the difference in bulb costs through changing your bulb less often. The electricity savings will go directly back into your budget.

- If your home has track lighting—lighting with multiple bulbs in a row—save it for special occasions. Track lighting may look nice, but it uses a lot of electricity—especially if you use incandescent (traditional) light bulbs instead of fluorescents. Turn these lights off immediately when you leave the room.

- Buy smaller lamps that use only one bulb for daily use.

- Open your blinds during the day to let in natural light.

- Put your lighting on a timer. This is a great option for those who have a tendency to leave lights on when they go to bed, or if you have a home office that is only used during the day. You can buy a timer inexpensively at any home store.

- According to the Department of Energy, 15 percent of your energy usage can be caused by energy leaks. If you are renting an apartment, check your windows and doors for light shining through and ask your landlord for window caulking and weather stripping when needed. If you own your home, you can pick up weather stripping at any home store and do the job yourself.

By making some or all of these changes, you could save anywhere from a few dollars per month on your electric bill to over $100. The exact amount you save depends on the area where you live and which changes you make.

You can also save money on your monthly electric bill by making a few other simple changes, such as using blackout curtains, learning how to utilize your ceiling fan to save money in the winter and summer, and buying inexpensive items such as a new air filter.

BLACKOUT CURTAINS

Curtains can save you money in two ways. First, knowing when to open and close your curtains will save you beaucoup bucks on your heating or cooling bill. How? During the winter, opening your blinds or curtains during the day to let in the sun helps to heat your home. Closing your blinds or curtains at night helps to keep the cold air out. In the summer, the opposite is true. Closing blinds or curtains during the day keeps excess heat out, while opening blinds or curtains at night lets cooler air in.

For optimum energy-saving effect, get blackout curtains. These curtains have an energy efficiency rating that rates the amount of heat or cool air blocked from outside. Another benefit to buying blackout curtains (versus investing money into energy-efficient windows or insulation) is their portability. If you live in an apartment or don't feel like you are going to spend at least another five years in a home, you can take your investment with you. Just pick neutral colors or patterns with a variety of colors, so your new drapes will fit in at your next home or if you decide to change your décor. And you don't have to buy all your curtains at once—or your light bulbs, for that matter. Change curtains and light bulbs in the rooms where they matter most. Bedrooms are a great place to start because you need lighting the most at night and you won't reset your heat or air conditioning in the middle of the night.

CEILING FANS

You'd love to keep your heater at 72 degrees in the winter because you're getting tired of wearing a sweater inside your home or stepping out of the shower onto a cold bathroom floor. In the summer, you would be happy to cool your home below 80 degrees because you're tired of sweating when you're inside your house. What do you do when you want to keep your electric bill down, but you're just uncomfortable in your own home? Use a ceiling fan.

Ceiling fans help a room feel cool, but they can actually keep the room warm and keep your heating bill down, too. In fact, ceiling fans can make a room feel a couple of degrees cooler or warmer, depending on how the fan is used.

In the summer, the clockwise motion of your fan blades circulate the cool air. I didn't notice that I could flip a switch so that the fan blades move in the other direction. I did so because my roommate at the time insisted on keeping the heater at 70 and it was just too cold. So I did some research on the Department of Energy Web site (http://energy. gov/energysaver) and found that if I flipped the fan's switch, the room would feel a couple of degrees warmer—and it did. I didn't have to change the temperature anymore when she left for work and then again before she came home.

There's a switch on the base of your fan to change direction of your fan blades. If you push this switch your fan blades will spin in the other direction and force warm air down instead of circulating cooler air around the room.

Always turn off ceiling fans when you leave the room. Your savings will be squashed if you substitute energy costs from the air conditioner with excessive ceiling fan usage. Plus, ceiling fans only work to make the room you are in more comfortable, so if you go to bed

Caution

Ceiling fans can have the opposite effect of what you want if they are switched in the wrong direction. Let's say you have your ceiling fan on, but the temperature doesn't feel any different than what your thermostat says. Turn your ceiling fan off and wait for the fan to stop. Then flip the switch. Turn the fan back and see if the room temperature feels better after about 5 minutes.

and leave the ceiling fan on in the living room, it won't do anything to help you.

Turn off lights on ceiling fans when you are using natural light in your home or use small lamps instead. In general, ceiling fans can use up to four separate bulbs. If you don't need that much light, using a lamp with one bulb or opening your blinds while you use your ceiling fan with its light switch turned off will save you a few bucks a month of electricity.

OTHER WAYS TO SAVE

Dirty air filters cause your air conditioner to work harder. Changing an air filter will cost you less than $10. If you live in an apartment you can call maintenance and they'll change your air filter for free.

If you live in an older home with odd-sized filters, there are numerous Web sites where you can order custom filters. Compare prices with at least three dealers and check with the Better Business Bureau (www.bbb.org) to make sure there are few or no customer complaints on the company you choose to order from.

No matter how efficient your air conditioner and heater are, having an air leak is going to raise your electric bill. If you can see light around your exterior door or in windowsills, go get a roll of weather stripping from any home improvement store for less than $10.

Digital thermostats can have timers where you can set the temperature to be lower or higher during certain hours, such as when you are at work.

> ### Caution
>
> Consider the comfort of your pets when setting the temperature using a timer. You don't want to freeze or overheat the furry, feathered, or even scaled members of your family.

Checklist for General Energy-Saving Tips

✓ To optimize energy efficiency without spending a dime, open your curtains during the day in the winter to let in natural light and heat from the sun to reduce heating bills.

✓ Don't run your ceiling fan when you are not in the room. It will add to your electric bill because you only feel the temperature difference in the room where the ceiling fan is on.

✓ Set your thermostat two degrees higher in the summer and two degrees lower in the winter than you normally would to soak up the energy savings.

✓ When using your ceiling fan during the day, pull the cord to turn off the lighting portion of your ceiling fan, especially if your curtains or blinds are open to let in natural light.

✓ Before thinking about which blackout curtains you'd like to purchase, budget for the exact amount you'd like to spend.

✓ When you buy blackout curtains, look for the Energy R-Value. Blackout curtains are rated the same way windows are rated for energy efficiency.

✓ Don't buy blackout curtains for every room if you can't afford it. Start with the rooms facing east or west. These are the rooms most exposed to the sun.

✓ Choose neutral colors, especially if you plan on moving in the next five years. This way your curtains will fit in with your new décor as well.

✓ Changing air filters as needed is one of the cheapest ways to save on electricity and potential air conditioner repairs.

Energy Audits

Energy auditors charge a fee to come out to your home and evaluate where you could change your energy habits and save money, but many electric companies will do this at no charge as a service to their customers.

What can an energy auditor find that you wouldn't? I had the energy auditor from the electric company come out to my home—for free—to perform an energy audit. The air conditioner wasn't functioning properly, and it turned out it needed a basic cleaning and a minor repair. Had I not had the energy audit, I would have spent hundreds more over the summer because the air conditioner would have to work harder—use more electricity—to function properly.

Energy auditors are specialists in saving you money. You may not think of all the energy wasters they encounter every day. Plus, they have special equipment that people don't normally have. According to the Energy Star Web site (www.energystar.gov), energy auditors use high-tech equipment such as infrared cameras to help find energy leaks and to determine how bad the leaks are. My energy auditor revealed energy leaks around my windows. I bought a few dollars' worth of caulk and sealed them right up.

To calculate energy savings by zip code, go to the Home Energy Saver Web site at http://hes.lbl.gov/.

Checklist for Energy Audits

✓ Ask your electric company to send an energy auditor out to your home for a free evaluation.

✓ Caulk or use weather stripping where air leaks exist.

✓ Fix appliances that may not be working properly.

✓ Ask your energy auditor how much savings you can achieve by completing each suggestion. This way you can evaluate what actions will save you the most money with the least amount of expense.

✓ If you live in a rented property, use the information you gather to contact your property manager with maintenance requests.

Fuel-Saving Tips

You have no idea when you last had the oil changed on your car, and you're running late to work. Each traffic light you have to stop at represents having to explain to your boss why you just can't just wake up ten minutes earlier, so you step hard on the gas pedal and burn a little more gasoline by going full throttle.

Gas prices go up, and gas prices go down. But either way, you can always save money by using less gas. And depending on which tips you follow, you won't even have to drive less:

• Plan your trips based on avoiding rush hour. The most frustrating and useless way to burn gas is to sit in stopped traffic. If you can leave 15 to 30 minutes earlier for work to experience less traffic congestion, do it. You can sit and have a bagel while reading a magazine before you start work. If you can change your schedule to avoid traffic congestion, that's even better.

• How fast you accelerate affects your gas mileage. Ease on and off your gas pedal to squeeze out a couple more miles per gallon of gasoline.

• Cruise control saves you money in two ways. First, your accelerator gets a break because you maintain a consistent speed; second, you are much less likely to get a speeding ticket, which would cost you a lot more than a tank or two of gasoline.

• No matter how tempted you are to get off the highway if there's traffic ahead, you normally get better gas mileage on highways than traveling on city roadways when you are going more than a few miles.

- Basic maintenance such as changing spark plugs and air filters at recommended intervals (see the following section) will make your car run better and thus increase your gas mileage.

- Using your vent instead of air conditioning when possible can increase your gas mileage as well.

Car Maintenance Schedules

It seems like your car breaks down every other week—and along with the repair comes a bill for a couple hundred dollars or more. Does it mean you should trade in your car for something that runs without fail, or go green and take public transport? Or should you just resign yourself to paying repair bills?

The answer may be none of the above. You just need to get on a regular maintenance schedule with a reliable mechanic. Just like if you skipped going to the dentist for years on end and thus developed cavities, your car needs a doctor's visit to prevent cavities in its radiator hose.

1. Find a reliable mechanic and have him evaluate your car's maintenance state. Go to the Better Business Bureau Web site (www.bbb.org) for help in finding a reliable mechanic. Check if the repair shop has had customer complaints and if so, how they've been resolved.

2. Ask questions:
   - What are the likely repairs based on the mileage and condition of your car? Likely repairs are as important as actual and impending repairs because it will give you a clue as to what expenses you could have in the future.

   - What repairs and regular maintenance are coming up?

   - What does your car need to perform at its best?

   - Will they send reminders in the mail or by phone when regular maintenance is due?

   - Do they work on a lot of cars of your make and model?

   - What kind of oil do they use?

3. Find out if your car is inches from a costly engine repair. Could your car just use a little maintenance sprucing, such as new spark plugs, distilled instead of regular water in your radiator, or a fluid change?

The following table shows how lack of some basic maintenance can cost you hundreds to thousands of dollars.

Basic Maintenance Item	Average Costs of Basic Maintenance	Cost of Repair
Oil changes	$80/per year	Anywhere from $1,500 to several thousand for an engine that wears out
Checking tire pressure	Free	Anywhere from $200 to $3,000 to replace tires, based on the model of your car
Filling your radiator with distilled water when water level is low	$.69	Over $100 for a new radiator, plus labor

Note: Costs may vary based on region of the country and make/model of vehicle.

Here are some simple things you can do to reduce vehicle repair bills:

- Learn how to check your car's fluid levels. You don't want an oil leak or low water level in your radiator to turn into hundreds of dollars in repairs. If you don't know how to check fluids, ask for help at your neighborhood auto parts store.

- Read your car's maintenance manual. Every car has a service manual that tells you when all basic maintenance is due. Not performing basic maintenance can invalidate your warranty. Why? If you were working in a retail shop, would you accept a returned vacuum that you were told didn't work if you found out the vacuum had been accidentally dropped down a staircase? Unless the warranty allowed for accident breakage, you wouldn't.

- Wash and wax your car regularly to maintain the condition of the paint. You may not want to get a new car as quickly if your current car is still in great condition.

Checklist for Car Maintenance

✓ Find a reliable mechanic who you use for all your car maintenance. Ask for referrals from friends or check for complaint history on the Better Business Bureau Web site (www.bbb.org).

✓ Perform regular maintenance as scheduled in your owner's manual. Performing regular maintenance prevents costly repairs.

✓ Learn how to check your vehicle's fluid levels. Ask the staff at your local auto parts store if you need help.

✓ Wash and wax your car regularly to keep it looking spiffy.

Saving Money on Commuting

Do you use public transit on a regular basis, but pay for it each time you use it? To evaluate whether to buy a monthly pass, start by calculating what you are spending now. You can estimate based on one week what you would spend in a month.

For example, Jane rides the subway five times a week for $5 each day, round-trip. She spends $25 per week times four, which equals $100 per month. The current cost of the unlimited ride card for the New York City public transit's unlimited 30-day pass is $112 per month. In this case, Jane would spend more if she bought a monthly pass than she does paying per subway token. However, if she went across town on weekends using the subway, she would save money by buying a monthly pass. This is because she'd spend another $10 going round-trip per weekend. Her cost without the pass would be $140.

There are also ways to get discounts in major cities when you don't buy rides in bulk. When I do use the subway, I use a reusable Metro-Card, which drops every one-way trip by $0.25 by using a MetroCard instead of single ride tickets from $2.75 to $2.50. Plus the MetroCard, which only costs a dollar, includes a 5 percent bonus for all monies added to the card. I only spend $40 per month on transportation, including a cab ride. D.C. also offers reusable card discounts on their Metro rail system.

This goes to show whether bulk passes work for you is very individualized, and you should calculate your expenses before deciding whether to buy massive passes on mass transit.

However, there are great alternatives to using public transportation. For example, if Jane lives within a few blocks of work, why hop on the subway when she can walk to work or ride a bicycle?

I chose a gym within a 20-minute walk from my home. I never take the subway to get there. After all, avoiding exercise to go somewhere to exercise defeats the purpose. Plus, I save $100 by avoiding 20 round trips per month. That more than pays for my membership!

If you don't have access to public transportation and aren't within a mile or two of work, consider carpooling with a coworker. It's not just about saving gas. Splitting commuting fees can be especially helpful if parking downtown is $5 or $10 per day—or if there happens to be toll charges along the way to work. Driving in the carpool lane can also save you quite a bit of time during rush hour. Plus, with someone else depending on you for a ride, you'll start a buddy system for making sure you get to work on time.

Checklist for Saving Money on Commuting

✓ Are you riding or driving a couple of blocks when you could walk or ride a bicycle the same distance?

✓ Do you use mass transit enough to warrant buying a bulk use pass?

✓ Have you compared the difference in price based on your individual habits?

✓ If mass transit isn't feasible where you live, have you considered carpooling?

Moving Closer to Work

Moving closer to work can solve two problems: transportation costs and long commutes. However, it can create problems if moving costs are high, the new neighborhood's rental prices are much higher than your old neighborhood, or you find another job you like better.

The first consideration in moving closer to work is to make sure your job is stable. One of the worst decisions you can make is to move before you know if you like your new job—or months before you switch jobs or get laid off. To avoid this precarious situation, ask yourself the following questions:

• Have you held your current position for at least six months?

• Have you heard any layoff or merger rumors? Do you have reason to believe any of them may be true?

• Have you had any performance reprimands in the last couple of months?

- Does the company you work for seem to be doing pretty well as far as keeping big clients?

There's not a definitive answer to how stable your job is, but answering these questions will make you feel a lot more comfortable about your decision to move.

In addition to the stability of your current position, consider moving costs and rent differences. To evaluate whether the moving costs are worth it, you need to calculate the total cost of moving and then divide it by the number of months in your lease and add it to the cost of your potential new rent.

Also remember to look at energy efficiency. Look for Energy Star appliances, and compare electricity costs between your new place and your old place by asking the new landlord or the new electric company about average monthly electricity costs for that particular apartment. Of course, there are exceptions. If you are moving out of state for a new career, obviously you can't keep your old pad.

Remember, these are mainly economic factors to a move, and you should weigh in your own personal preferences when making the final decision—as long as your budget can handle it.

Checklist for Moving Closer to Work

✓ Evaluate the stability of your employment. Whether you are moving closer to a job you have been at for five years or one where you are newly employed, do not move unless you feel your job is stable.

✓ If it's a new job and it's within a 50-mile radius of where you live now, commute from your old place until you know you are happy and will stay in your new position.

✓ Add up rent and transportation to determine possible savings. You aren't saving money if your new rent cancels out any savings in transportation.

✓ Consider moving costs in relation to lease length. For instance, if you are signing a 12-month lease and your moving costs are $500, you need to add approximately $42 per month to your rent in order to compare it to your old apartment.

✓ Be extra careful when your move involves selling one home to buy another. Wait a couple more months before completing the move.

✓ Remember to look at the energy efficiency of your new place.

Chapter Wrap-Up

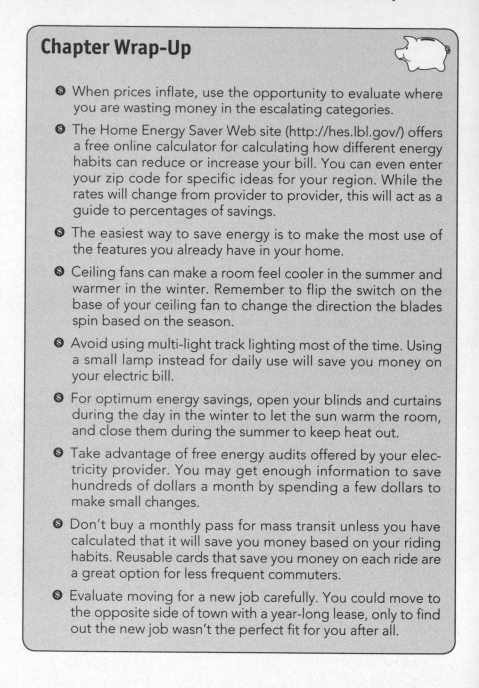

- When prices inflate, use the opportunity to evaluate where you are wasting money in the escalating categories.

- The Home Energy Saver Web site (http://hes.lbl.gov/) offers a free online calculator for calculating how different energy habits can reduce or increase your bill. You can even enter your zip code for specific ideas for your region. While the rates will change from provider to provider, this will act as a guide to percentages of savings.

- The easiest way to save energy is to make the most use of the features you already have in your home.

- Ceiling fans can make a room feel cooler in the summer and warmer in the winter. Remember to flip the switch on the base of your ceiling fan to change the direction the blades spin based on the season.

- Avoid using multi-light track lighting most of the time. Using a small lamp instead for daily use will save you money on your electric bill.

- For optimum energy savings, open your blinds and curtains during the day in the winter to let the sun warm the room, and close them during the summer to keep heat out.

- Take advantage of free energy audits offered by your electricity provider. You may get enough information to save hundreds of dollars a month by spending a few dollars to make small changes.

- Don't buy a monthly pass for mass transit unless you have calculated that it will save you money based on your riding habits. Reusable cards that save you money on each ride are a great option for less frequent commuters.

- Evaluate moving for a new job carefully. You could move to the opposite side of town with a year-long lease, only to find out the new job wasn't the perfect fit for you after all.

Budgeting Through Layoffs, Pay Cuts, and Career Changes

For a few months now you've heard rumors around the water cooler that there may be layoffs coming soon due to a drop in sales numbers at your company. Other rumors are flying around about pay cuts. You're unsure about whether you want to start looking for another job—especially when all you have to base your decision on is hearsay.

What can you do now? Get your budget and your savings in order so you can rebound from any financial change you may encounter. Many of my friends have had to deal with layoffs, and those who managed to get through the event as unscathed as possible cut their expenses. Those who didn't suffered emotional and financial distress.

By giving your savings a potential pre-layoff jolt, paying off credit cards or car loans early, avoiding new debt, and/or buying involuntary unemployment credit card insurance, you'll be able to prepare for a financial pitfall and rebound with barely a scuff mark on your best suit.

Jolt Your Savings

Ideally, it's good to have a six- to eight-month emergency fund, but most of us don't bounce out of school—or our twenties or thirties— with an instant savings of $10,000 or more. Even though your savings account is as small as you'd like your credit card balances to be, you can start building your savings now to save for the rainy days you suspect are ahead. Try these strategies for savings success.

GIVE YOURSELF A CLEAN SLATE

In the past you may have had a hard time saving money—maybe because you were working just enough to pay basic bills, more fun items got in the way of you saving, or putting aside six to eight months' worth seemed like too daunting a task. A clean slate is necessary to begin the process of going from being a spender to a saver. Forgive yourself right now for not saving as much as you should have. Make a list of the five things you think have been keeping you from creating an emergency fund, and then in the next column, write down how you are going to correct those habits. You can wait to fill in the changes side until you read on about savings strategies. Here's an example of what your list might look like.

Five Spending Habits That Have Prevented Me from Saving

1. I get bored easily and go shopping to kill time.
2. I have to buy something new to wear every time I go to a major event.
3. I have a big family or group of friends, and it's always someone's birthday.
4. My friends and I love to go the martini bar for $12 drinks.
5. I love buying fresh fruit and veggies, but half of what I buy always seems to spoil.

How I Am Going to Change These Habits

1. Find a hobby such as going to the gym that has a set membership fee each month that I can fit into my budget.
2. Buy accessories or a single piece of clothing that goes with clothing I already have.
3. Buy thoughtful gifts instead of pricey ones, such as a hand-held pastry blender for someone who has always wanted to make homemade pie crusts.
4. Still go out, but limit myself to one martini or two lower-priced drinks. I'll also avoid having to pay for cab fare home when I leave my car at the bar. (Finding a place where you won't have to pay

$12 per drink is helpful, too. In fact, choosing a different place once in awhile might cure #1 on your list, boredom. See Chapter 12, "Reaping the Rewards of a Frugal Lifestyle," for tips on saving money when dining out.)

5. Buy only the produce I think I'll need for the coming week, and consider how long each item takes to spoil. (For example, asparagus that's ready to eat may not last until the end of the week, and a bag of salad that expires in a couple of days shouldn't be bought in multiples. When in doubt of how long fruit or veggies last, ask the produce manager.)

PUT ASIDE A SET AMOUNT FROM EACH PAYCHECK INTO SAVINGS

Start with what you can safely spare from your budget right now that could go into your emergency savings account. For example, you bring home $2,000 per month and $1,800 is earmarked for your expenses. Stash the $200 difference between your income and your expenses into your savings account.

PUT TAX REFUND MONEY INTO SAVINGS

If you receive a tax refund each year, that money is not part of your regular budget. Put it into your savings account—especially if a possible layoff is on the horizon.

Checklist for Jolting Savings

✓ Look at your last two months of expenses and make sure you can afford to set aside money to go into your savings without charging more on your credit cards.

✓ If you don't have extra money available, look at what expenses you could trim to redirect that money to your savings account. For example, if you have a certain amount reserved each month toward changing your floors from carpet to hardwood throughout your house, redirect this money into savings or paying off debt. You can also do little things like buying lower-priced items in the grocery store or going out one less time per month and putting that amount into savings.

- Stash extra money from bonuses, extra paychecks, or tax refunds into your savings account. Especially if you've been living comfortably on your current salary, you can afford to take any extra money you receive and stash it into your emergency fund.

- Create a livable budget that includes money for all routine maintenance and repairs. Construct a bare-bones budget for layoffs and other financially skinny times that takes into account all necessities—including food, keeping a roof over your head, and having enough gas to get to and from work.

> **Caution**
>
> If you suspect you may be laid off, your first response may be to go into hyper-savings mode, but don't go overboard. Maybe you put every spare penny you have into your savings account and six months down the line you still have your job. However, while you were beefing up your savings account, you postponed fixing the water heater in your home, and now that initial $100 repair will cost $500 because of additional damages. You also skipped the scheduled car maintenance you needed that would have cost $400, which is now going to cost $2,000 in additional repairs. Don't sock away money for a rainy day at the expense of making necessary repairs.

Preventing Long-Term Damage from a Layoff

You just got laid off, and the $10,000 limit on your credit card is awfully appealing to help you maintain your lifestyle. Resist the urge to use your credit card to make up any income differences. Stick to your bare-bones budget until you can find another job.

Why?

A common strategy to get through a layoff or other financial speed bump is to rely on charge cards. However, even seemingly minimal charging can add up fast—$200 a month to cover a couple of your bills adds up to $1,200 in six months' time, and $500 a month adds up to $3,000. And that's without factoring in any interest.

Here's an example of how layoff credit card reliance can get you into trouble. Let's say you currently take home $2,400 per month. You get laid off, but you receive unemployment; it drops your pay to around

$1,200 per month. However, you don't change your budget and still spend like you were making $2,400 every month. Six months later you've rung up $7,200 of extra charges on your credit card. If your minimum monthly payment is 4 percent of the balance, you now have a $288 minimum payment. Almost $300 per month of extra expenses is going to impact your budget, whether you've already found a new job or not.

Preventing long-term damage from a layoff is a result of developing a solid plan for how to get through this temporary period of your life. Keep your eye on the prize of a financially secure future. Keep credit card spending to an absolute minimum. Calculate each month what your payments would be on your credit cards and your total debt.

Other financially challenging situations include taking a pay cut or accepting a lower-paying job that's more rewarding or has a more flexible schedule. Think about your current budget and debt situation, and use similar strategies to adjust your budget for the following situations:

- **Returning to school.** You've reduced your work hours or stopped working altogether. You may have also changed jobs to a part-time job that is low-paying or an internship that has no pay.

- **Injury or short-term disability.** While a layoff is at least somewhat predictable based on the state of the economy, your company, or your industry, a short- or long-term disability—especially from a work place incident—is not.

- **Reduced pay.** If your salary gets cut by 10 percent, you've got to live accordingly.

You can get through any of these situations, but it will take some budgeting elbow grease. Start spending less now to prepare for financially difficult situations.

Checklist for Credit Card Spending During Tough Financial Situations

✓ Keep credit charges to a minimum (this is a good policy whether you get laid off or not).

✓ Look at the total amount you owe each month on your credit card instead of just the minimum payment.

✓ Remember, you will be paying for your layoff for years if you live on your credit card.

The Bare-Bones Budget

When you feel stable in your life, you can go by a budget that allows for almost all of your needs and wants—within reason. After all, even in good times, you need a little room in your budget for emergency savings and unexpected situations.

But when circumstances force you to start looking at cutting your lattes, even though you've already cut down on going out for Happy Hour and deleted some of your favorite items from your grocery budget, you just have to do it for the sake of long-term sanity. Try some of these tips to figure out how you could cut back before an unexpected situation happens:

- Look at your personal must-haves list and your grocery list and see if there are any items that are normally personal necessities that could turn into luxuries when money is tight.

- Consider whether your basic expenses are reasonable, and if not, if they are fixable. Are you including all the movie channels as a basic and necessary expense? Show caution in what is absolutely necessary.

- Make your savings relatively inaccessible. Any account with money in it that isn't going toward bills is tempting to dive into when you get the urge for an emergency weekend getaway, shopping trip, or special date. But your savings account is only useful if you define what qualifies as a need, and how much access you can have and still follow your defined withdrawal rules.

- Stave off purchasing anything that's not necessary—especially big purchases such as furniture, cars, major remodeling work, and so on—until you feel safe from the possibility of layoffs for at least six months. The last thing you want to do is either deplete your savings account or add to your credit debt and payments by making a major purchase when you may not have a job in six months. Weigh each purchase carefully.

Go through the budget you created in Chapter 5, "Budgeting for Your Lifestyle and Your Loans," and pick at least five categories where you could cut spending. Of course, you want to cut empty spending like overspending on car insurance first.

Make a list of these five expenses, and then below write what you are going to do to trim the expense. For example:

Dining out

Prepare at least one more meal a week myself instead of eating lunch out on a daily basis.

Go through your whole budget to see where cuts can be made. It's much less painful to create a bare-bones budget now, before it becomes a necessity, than it is to create one in a reduced-pay situation.

Checklist for Creating a Bare-Bones Budget

✓ Have a budget prepared now that only includes your basic expenses.

✓ Identify five expenses you can cut down on if a layoff occurred.

✓ Don't neglect basic car or home maintenance. A car or home that's poorly maintained could result in large bills that you can't afford to pay.

✓ Have rules for when to take money out of savings. You could be laid off for a long time. You may need your money at a later date more than you do now.

Use Loan Forbearance Sparingly

It's always tempting during a financially challenging time to request forbearance or deferment on your federal student loans, but there are two problems with using these options as a crutch:

- **Economic deference is generally limited and some forbearance types are awarded at the discretion of the individual lenders.**

- **Your interest can grow during temporary reprieves using forbearance.** You aren't getting a break from what you owe from your loans, you are only putting on hold repayment while interest accrues. For example, let's say you have $60,000 in student debt at a rate of 5 percent. You decide to take a six-month break from student loans. At the end of six months you've extended your payments by six months and you now owe $61,500. You'll either have to repay the interest you've accrued before the six months end, or the rest of your payments will increase by a few dollars every month because of the increased amount you now owe. The government may pay your interest if you qualify for a deferment, but not forbearance. Check with your servicer for current deferment qualifications.

Use forbearance and deferments sparingly so that you don't wake up with double your student loan debt one day. See Chapter 2, "Organizing Your Student Debt Payments," for more on forbearance and deferment.

Checklist for Using Forbearance

✓ Know your limits: generally three years of economic deferment.

✓ Use forbearance only when necessary.

✓ Have a plan for making your student loan payments when your approved forbearance time period ends.

Paying Down Credit Card and Loan Balances

You know a change in your career is coming, and while you've had no problem managing your money with your current salary, you know a drop in salary would cause a serious cash shortage. How do you prepare when you know your lifestyle can't be maintained at a lower level?

Remember all the money you put into paying down student loans? Redirect the same amount to paying off your other loans. In general, it's always best to put extra money toward your highest-interest loans first. This includes student loans, mortgages, personal loans, and credit card debts.

But when you are preparing for a layoff or a time period where you aren't going to have as much money to pay your bills, it's important to pay the smallest balances first. Why? Because it gets rid of one bill.

For example, let's say you have credit balances of $500, $1,000, and $2,500. In addition, you have a five-year, $15,000 car loan with six months left. Your monthly payments on your credit cards are $15, $30, and $75. Your monthly car payment is $283. Obviously, getting rid of your car payment would free up the most cash in your budget, but even $15 makes a dent in your monthly bills.

Here's how this example looks in table form. Create your own chart similar to this one to analyze what debts you could pay off before a possible layoff.

Loan	Months Left	Budget Demand	Total to Pay Off
Car loan	6	$283*	$1,668
Credit card 1	Revolving debt	$15	$500
Credit card 2	Revolving debt	$30	$1,000
Credit card 3	Revolving debt	$75	$2,500

*The car payment is calculated at a 5 percent interest rate. The payoff amount is a little less than six times the payment amount because of the interest that you wouldn't have to pay if you paid off the loan earlier.

Emergency funds aren't just about having savings set aside to pay bills if you lose your job, your car breaks down, or you have medical expenses. You also need to think about emergency spending—having a budget that's slimmed down to accommodate less money coming in. The easiest way to do this is start paying off recurring bills.

For instance, how close are you to having your credit cards paid off? Could you pay them off in the next few months on your present salary, while jolting your savings? Is your car loan within a few months of being paid off?

When a friend suspected a temporary layoff, his car loan had a few payments left. He cut down extra spending and paid off his car loan before his layoff hit.

Here's one thing to be aware of. Let's say you pay six months' worth of principal ahead on your car loan prior to a layoff, but you have nine months total left on the loan. You sacrificed some of your savings to make the payments ahead, so now you have less money in your savings and no job. Plus, you still have three months of payments left on your car loan. Paying six months ahead in this situation was a bad idea because you will still have a loan payment during a layoff.

Caution

The absolute worst thing—or at least, among the top worst things—that you could do with your money is to pay off one credit card just so you can later regrow it when you can't afford your payments. Even when you are worried about an upcoming layoff, you don't want to pay off debt and then have so tight a budget that you start charging on your credit cards to pay your monthly bills.

You can't always predict when you are going to get laid off, get a pay cut, or change careers. But if you see signs that your company is about to cut jobs, reduce pay, or you decide to move on to another company or profession, it's time to start preparing for the potential financial fallout before it happens.

Checklist for Paying Down Debt Prior to a Layoff

✓ Avoid looking solely at balances owed to determine which would cut the most off of your total bill payments. Look at both interest rates and balances owed. Why? Let's say you have one card with a $500 balance and one card with a $2,000 balance. Even if the $500 card has a higher interest rate, you could eliminate a credit card payment if you paid it off.

✓ Set goals based on when you expect the career change or layoff: six months, three months, or one month. If you have only one month, obviously it's going to be harder to plan.

✓ Don't pay off a credit card only to start charging on your credit card again just to pay all your bills. For example, you paid off your card with a $2,000 balance just prior to your layoff. You wiped out your savings account to do it. Now, you have to use your credit cards to make up for the money you needed during your layoff that was in your savings account.

✓ Think carefully about which strategies you choose to get through a layoff situation. They can vary widely from person to person based on individual expenses.

Involuntary Unemployment Credit Card Insurance

Every time you get a new credit card or you activate a replacement card, your credit card company tries to sell you involuntary unemployment insurance on your credit card. But do you need it, and will it cost you more in the long run than making your credit card payments?

Most credit card companies offer an insurance policy for unexpected circumstances such as unemployment, death, disability, or loss of property.

Here's how it works. If you become unemployed, your credit card's insurance company will pick up the tab for your minimum payment until you find a new job or until the time limit of the benefit wears out. The charges vary, but usually it is 1 percent of your monthly balance. For example, if you are currently carrying a balance of $1,000, your unemployment insurance would cost you $10 per month; $2,000 would cost you $20 per month; and $5,000 would cost you $50 per month.

Compare the price of insurance to your minimum payment of 3 percent of your balance, which would be $30 on a $1,000 balance, or $150 on a $5,000 balance. As you can see, you'd save quite a bit if you get laid off.

> **Caution**
>
> In order to qualify for involuntary unemployment credit card insurance, you have to lose your job in such a way that you would qualify for state unemployment insurance, which leaves this benefit useless for anyone who is self-employed.

However, the insurance can be pricey if you end up keeping your job, because in three months of making insurance payments you will have thrown away a full month's payment on your credit card. At that rate you could work toward paying off your credit cards early with extra payments or save to make payments in case of layoff.

So if you're unsure of whether you're going to get laid off, how do you decide if unemployment insurance is worth it on your credit cards?

Have you been given or seen a WARN letter posted? WARN (Worker Adjustment and Retraining Notification Act) letters are often issued when large companies are about to do a massive layoff to give 60 days' notice to employees. In certain situations and sizes of layoffs it is a requirement from the federal government through the 1989 legislation of the Worker Adjustment and Retraining Notification Act.

If your company falls within the WARN letter guidelines and the layoff isn't due to certain exempted occurrences such as a natural disaster, like a tornado obliterating a factory, you will either see a letter posted or your union, if you are represented by one, will distribute the information to you.

Both management and all other positions that are included in a massive layoff are subject to WARN letters. For more information on WARN letters, check out the United States Department of Labor Web site (www.doleta.gov/layoff/warn.cfm).

If you don't see a WARN letter posted, then go with your gut when predicting or planning for potential layoffs and deciding when it's time to buy involuntary unemployment credit card insurance.

Checklist for Buying Involuntary Unemployment Credit Card Insurance

✓ Figure out how close you are to paying off your credit cards. If you could pay off your cards in the next few months, especially if you don't think a layoff is coming soon, you can avoid buying involuntary unemployment credit card insurance.

✓ Calculate how many months it would take of being laid off to make up the difference of each payment you make to involuntary unemployment credit card insurance.

✓ Determine the likelihood that you will get laid off in the near future. If it's unlikely you will get laid off in the next two to four months, you shouldn't need involuntary unemployment credit card insurance yet.

✓ If you don't choose to get involuntary unemployment credit card insurance, start building your savings account to add up to enough money to pay your credit cards and other bills for at least six months.

✓ If you suspect a layoff, call your state's unemployment office to find out approximately what your benefits would be and what the maximum processing time would be to receive benefits. This will tell you if you'll be able to afford your payments and give you an idea of how long you could go between your last paycheck and an unemployment check.

Chapter Wrap-Up

$ Before budgeting for any layoff situation, start by looking at the sum total of your debts, including current payments and total balances. You can't formulate a plan to tackle a problem unless you know exactly what your total debt is.

$ Jolt your savings before a layoff so you have a thick money cushion to land on in the event it occurs.

$ Determine which debts you could pay off the soonest and work on paying those off first.

$ Make a commitment to how you are going to prepare for potential layoffs by identifying five things you are willing to do now to save money.

$ Have a bare-bones budget in place so you can avoid making decisions when your state of mind is not the best—right after a layoff or when your pay is cut.

$ Don't create an automatic "fountain of youth" for reviving your debt. Your goal should be to budget for possibilities but not hurt your current or future reality by increasing credit card debt.

⑤ If you do add debt to your credit card, keep it to a minimum and perpetually calculate the time it will take you to pay it off.

⑤ Evaluate involuntary unemployment credit card insurance based on what you can afford, how long it will take you to pay it off on your own, and the monthly cost.

⑤ Go to www.doleta.gov/layoff/warn.cfm to read about layoff WARN letters regulated by the government through the Worker Adjustment and Retraining Notification Act.

⑤ Don't wait until a layoff is imminent before you develop an unemployment contingency plan. Have your plan ready now, so that if you do encounter financial troubles later you can plan for your next job carefully without having to make rush decisions when you are in panic mode.

Paying Off Your Student Loans Early

Ready to get your student loan debt off your back, but you don't happen to have $40,000 or more lying around? You can cut years off of your payment schedule while barely making a dent in your monthly budget.

Paying off student loans early doesn't have to mean scrimping and saving to make double payments. There are numerous ways paying a few extra dollars a month can make years of difference in when your student loans are paid off.

Adding Money to Your Loan Payments

Your student loans have been weighing on your life for way longer than you'd care to admit. You'd love to not have to deal with them for another 10, 20, or 30 years, but you don't have the $80,000 on hand to pay off your loans. So start small by adding $5, $10, or $20 to your monthly payment.

How could as little as five bucks a month help you pay off your student loans faster? The amount you owe will be reduced by each $5 you add to your payments, but you'll also reduce your total bill by the interest you would be charged on that amount of money. For example, at a 6 percent interest rate for 30 years, $5 of your loan would cost almost $24 to borrow. That's three times your payment! Think about how much you'd save by paying $5 extra every month.

Now, not every $5 will save you $24 in interest. This is because if you have a higher interest rate, you are charged more in interest to borrow that $5. If you have a lower interest rate you are charged less.

Check out the following table to see how making additional small monthly payments in year five of these consolidated loans would make a difference in how fast the loans are paid off.

	Time Saved Off Loan by Adding $5 per Month	Time Saved Off Loan by Adding $10 per Month	Time Saved Off Loan by Adding $20 per Month
$50,000 consolidated at 4% (25-year loan)	9 months	18 months	34 months
$60,000 consolidated at 4% (30-year loan)	11 months	22 months	42 months
$70,000 consolidated at 5% (30-year loan)	10 months	20 months	38 months
$80,000 consolidated at 5% (30-year loan)	9 months	18 months	34 months

Checklist for Adding Small Payments

✓ Commit to only making extra payments you can afford. Small payments can make a huge difference in the time it takes to pay off your loan. Don't charge daily expenses on your credit card in order to make the extra payments, however. It's not worth it and will cost you more in the long run.

✓ Look at your budget to determine the exact amount you should spend on extra payments.

Caution

While adding small payments will help you pay off your loans more quickly, it will not save you money if you do it at the expense of other items in your budget. Don't skip a payment on your credit card or charge a daily expense in order to pay extra on your student loan. Only make extra payments you can painlessly afford.

✓ If you have a consolidation loan that requires a set number of payments to achieve your borrower benefits, put the extra $5 or $10 into a savings account to put toward your loan once your borrower benefits have been achieved.

Biweekly Loan Payments

You get paid every two weeks, but all your bills are monthly, including your student loan payments. But as with any interest-bearing debt, you could pay off your student loans faster if you made halved, biweekly payments and it would feel exactly the same on your budget; for example, paying $150 every two weeks instead of $300 per month.

Why don't biweekly payments dent your budget? For anyone with biweekly paychecks, your budget is based on getting two paychecks per month. However, twice a year, you'll get an extra paycheck, which means that's extra money to reduce debt, save for a vehicle, or rainy-day emergency money.

How does your loan get paid off faster with biweekly payments? In two ways: If your loan payment is divided in half and you pay it every two weeks, you are making 26 biweekly payments. Divide that by two to get the number of months worth of payments you are making, and you are making 13 months of payments—one more than the 12 months you would normally pay.

An alternative way to do this so you can keep your direct debit discount is to pay your monthly payments as usual, and then make an extra half payment when you get three checks in one month. For example, if you get paid on the 1st, 15th, and 31st of May, you would take half of your student loan payment out of your May 31st paycheck, and send in to your servicer as an extra payment.

If you have borrower benefits that you haven't achieved yet, you want to save the extra half payments in a savings account. Send in the money you've saved as one payment once your borrower benefits are earned and confirmed.

Caution

Watch when you start making biweekly payments. Always start this plan two weeks after your last payment paid on the due date, otherwise you could end up with a late payment because you would be paying a half payment on your due date. Also, keep in mind that making extra payments alone may not void your borrower benefit terms, but saving them up instead of paying the extra money now prevents any computer errors in keeping track of your payments. Keep the process simple.

Checklist for Biweekly Payments

✓ Look at the dates of when your paychecks come in and pinpoint when you could make extra payments.

✓ Review your other bills, and make sure you don't have a higher-interest car loan, credit card, or mortgage that would be a better choice to pay extra on.

✓ If you have a consolidation benefit attached to your loan such as a lower interest rebate or cash rebate after a certain number of months, proceed with biweekly payments or extra payments cautiously. Put the money from the extra payments you would have made if you chose to do biweekly payments in a savings account. Then use that money to pay down your loan in one lump sum once you have confirmed in writing that you have earned your consolidation benefit.

✓ If you have a direct debit discount, use this method by making an extra half student loan payment when you get a third check in one month.

Direct Debit Interest Rate Deductions

Your student loan servicer offers you a .25 percent interest rate deduction to pay your student loan via automatic payments out of your bank account every month. Why does your servicer want to give you free money for paying your normal bill?

The theory is that if your bill comes out of your checking account every month, you are more likely to pay it. Thus, they won't have to spend time and money trying to collect your debt. The payments are the same, but you owe just a little less on your student loans every month, so your payoff becomes smaller and smaller.

Here's an example of how much this can help you. Let's say you have a consolidated loan of $50,000 at 4.5 percent. You sign up for direct debit and as long as you have your payments direct debited, your interest rate is reduced to 4.25 percent. You just started making payments and you have 25 years left. Your payment is $277.92 regardless of whether you have this interest rate deduction or not. However, with the .25 percent interest deduction, you'd pay off your loan in just under 24 years.

Here's how direct debit works. You fill out a form that you either download from your servicer's Web site or that your servicer sends you in the mail. After a month or two your payment starts coming out of your checking or savings account, whichever one you chose on your direct debit form. Until your direct debit officially starts, you will want to continue making payments by mail, phone, or online.

The catch is in the paperwork and the paper trail. When you sign up for direct debit, you have to be careful not to miss a payment while your paperwork is being processed. You also have to remember to fill out new forms when you change bank accounts.

You don't want to lose a benefit from your consolidation or have a missed payment pop up on your credit report when you have this amount already in your monthly budget.

Here's a month-by-month example of how missing a payment due to direct debit can get you in trouble.

January

- You sign up for direct debit and fill out your form.

- You go ahead and make a manual payment.

February

- You receive a letter in the mail that your form has been received.

- You assume your payment via direct deposit has been received and forgo making a manual payment.

March

- Around the first of the month you notice your bank account has more money in it than you expected.

- You call up your servicer and find out your direct debit payment didn't get deducted in February but will in March.

- You make the February payment manually, but you now have a ding against your credit and you're no longer in contention to receive your consolidation benefits.

End of March

- You ask to be reinstated in the program to earn your consolidation benefits, but you have to wait to see if you get a letter from your student loan company.

April/May

- You get a response of yes or no to the reinstatement of your ability to earn your consolidation benefit.

This example could happen several times due to servicer changes where new direct debit forms have to be filed, you change bank accounts, or you go through a period of unemployment where your money isn't coming in at the same time—or at all.

If you encounter financial difficulty of any kind, remember to ask for forbearance or deferment (see Chapter 2, "Organizing Your Student Debt Payments") and wait for notification of approval before missing any payments.

Direct debit is a phenomenal—and free—way to pay off your student debt earlier. But you do have to be a little more cautious and follow the paper trails.

Checklist for Direct Debit Interest Rate Deduction

✓ Make sure your direct debit form is processed with your servicer before stopping manual payments.

✓ Fill out a new form when you change bank accounts or your loan has been transferred to another bank.

✓ Don't stop making payments if you're granted forbearance or deferment until you have confirmation of approval for your temporary payment reprieve—and you know exactly what payment coincides with the beginning of your forbearance or deferment.

✓ Remember to check your account to make sure your payment is deducted.

Student Loan Interest Tax Deduction

You'd love to pay off your student debt early if it weren't for one thing standing in the way—all the other bills you have to pay on a regular basis. The student loan interest tax deduction is the best thing that ever happened to debt-overloaded college grads. It's one of the few deductions you can take, as long as you qualify, without having to itemize deductions. Itemizing deductions is when you have so many tax-deductible items in your life such as home mortgages that you tally up your tax deductions instead of taking the standard personal deduction everyone gets to take.

If you don't know whether you're better off taking the standard deduction or itemizing, try the free tax software available on the IRS Web site (www.irs.gov) or through tax program Web sites such as turbotax.com. It will figure out what you can deduct by asking you questions about your financial life.

Depending on your income and the amount of interest you paid on your student loans, you could get back hundreds of dollars at the end of the year in your tax refund check. The money you get back could be used as a nice chunk of change toward paying off your student debt. You can also adjust your withholdings to get this extra cash in your paycheck throughout the year. (For more on adjusting withholding, see Chapter 2, which also goes over how to get your money back for previous years in which you didn't declare the deduction you earned.)

Here's how it works. The student loan interest tax deduction takes your student loan payments for the year and deducts them from your annual income. Thus, you're paying taxes on that much of your income.

For example, let's say you are single and made $60,000 last year. You have monthly student loan payments of $322, and the interest that you pay in a year's time adds up to about $2,400. You can now pay taxes on $57,600 (before subtracting your other deductions). Unless you adjusted your withholding on your W-4 form with your employer, you'll get a tax refund based on the amount of tax you paid on this money.

Is there a catch? The student loan interest tax deduction is relatively catchless. Both private and federal loans can qualify. You can file amended returns for the past three years to declare the deduction on past returns—and even get paid interest on the money from the IRS.

But there are two circumstances where you won't be able to make use of the deduction:

- **If your name is not on the loan.** For example, if your parents borrowed a parent plus loan and you make the payments, they are still the ones who can declare the tax deduction, and vice versa if they make your payments for you on loans in your name.

- **If your income is above the maximum allowed.** Each year, a maximum income amount is released for qualifying for the student loan tax deduction. You can find the amount for this year by going to the IRS Web site at www.irs.gov.

Checklist for Student Loan Interest Tax Deduction

✓ Consider the tax refund you get from your student loan interest tax deduction as money that should go toward paying off your loan.

✓ Refer to www.irs.gov for the income limit for the current tax year.

✓ You can declare your student loan interest tax deduction without itemizing deductions.

✓ You can make use of this deduction whether you have private or federal student loan debt.

✓ Don't throw away money. If you were eligible to declare your student loan interest tax deductions in past years but didn't, file amended returns.

Debunking Student Loan Interest and Other Tax Myths

Think the IRS only wants to collect money from your paycheck? Jim Southwell of the IRS shows you when and how you can pay less tax.

Myth: You must itemize deductions in order to deduct your student loan interest.

Fact: Assuming you meet the qualifications, you can deduct student loan interest without itemizing all your other deductions.

Myth: You can deduct student loan interest even if you got a really, really great job.

Fact: There are income limits that govern how much you can deduct for student loan interest. If your Modified Adjusted Gross Income (it's complicated, but usually close to the total amount of your income before any other deductions) was more than $60,000 ($125,000 if you're married and filing a joint return) for the 2012 tax year, then the amount you can deduct will start to phase out . . . and it could go to zero. But be happy—this just means that you really do have a great job! And, despite the higher marginal tax rates for higher incomes, you'll probably get to keep about two-thirds of the extra money you're making.

Myth: It's complicated to figure out at what point your student loan interest tax deduction is completely phased out.

Fact: It's actually pretty easy. You can find the phase-out range by reading IRS Publication 970 or searching for student loan interest deduction on www.irs.gov. Generally, it's $15,000 above the income limit for filing as a single person and $30,000 for filing a joint return as a married couple. Then how much you can deduct is based on how far over the limit you are.

For example, if you paid $1,800 in student loan interest in the 2009 tax year and you made $70,000, you would be able to declare a student loan interest tax deduction of $600. This was calculated by multiplying your student loan interest paid by the amount you are over the income limit divided by the phase-out period. For this example, the equation is:

$$\$1,800 \times (\$70,000 - \$60,000) \div \$15,000 = \$1,200$$

The deduction amount is then calculated: $1,800 − $1,200 = $600

Myth: All your loans qualify for a student loan interest tax deduction.

Fact: Only the interest you pay on loans taken out solely to pay for qualified education expenses qualifies.

Myth: It's difficult to figure out if you qualify for the student loan interest deduction if you are self-employed.

Fact: The rules are the same whether you are salaried or self-employed. The biggest variable for most self-employed people is that they may not know for sure until the end of the year whether their income is going to be more than the limit. You should definitely keep good records—especially the Form 1098-E showing how much interest you paid—and refer to it before you file your tax return.

Myth: Self-employed filers don't have to worry about underestimating taxes.

Fact: You can get penalized for not paying enough of your estimated taxes on your quarterly payment due dates. Since your income isn't likely to be a steady amount from year to year, you can vary your payments each quarter based on the income you earned that quarter or do the safe harbor approach. For most people, as long as you make quarterly payments equal to last year's payments, you won't owe a penalty. However, if your income was higher than last year, you will likely owe additional income tax.

Don't forget to input your student loan interest into the IRS withholdings calculator. This and your other allowances (such as your dependent children, or parents if you qualify to claim them as an exemption) will help you save money all year on your withheld taxes.

Workplace Bonuses and Salary Increases

You've done a great job of managing your student debt so far. Now, the career position you achieved through hard work and your education is finally panning out in the form of more money.

Since you've handled your expenses on less, you can still boost your lifestyle while putting part of your bonus or salary increase aside to help pay down your student loan debt.

One-time bonuses aren't something you should use for boosting your lifestyle. But you can use these to pay off some debt and take about 20 percent to buy something or take a vacation to reward yourself. Divide the rest between your savings account and making an extra payment toward your student loans.

There are some exceptions to using salary increases and one-time bonuses for paying down student loan debt:

- **You have credit card debt.** Credit card debt should always be paid off first before any federal student loan. Believe it or not, in addition to having the debt hanging over you, a $2,000 credit card balance can have more of an effect when applying for car or home loans than a $50,000 student loan. For example, if your maximum limit is $500 and you have a $200 balance, you're using 40 percent of your available credit on your card. With a $200 payment, you'd bring your utilization rate on this particular card down to 0 percent.

- **You want to buy a house soon and are getting ready for the extra expenses or to make a down payment.** A workplace bonus is perfect for putting money into your savings account for a down payment. However, if you are buying a home because of a salary increase, you should wait to make extra student loan payments until you've managed your new home expenses for at least six months.

- **You have less than $1,000 in your savings account.** In this case, it might be better to build up your emergency fund to at least a thousand or two before working on paying off your student loan debt.

Checklist for Bonuses and Pay Increases

✓ Pay off credit card debt first.

✓ Since bonuses are not part of your monthly budget, use at least half of this money toward paying off credit cards, student loan debt, or to put into a savings account.

✓ If you plan on buying a home in the next two years, funnel the extra money toward what will help you the most for buying your home. If you have high credit card debt, pay that off first. If you don't, funnel the money toward your down payment.

✓ If you get a pay raise, increase your lifestyle and decrease your debt slowly. For example, if you buy a home, wait on buying a new car or making extra student loan payments until you've handled your new expenses for at least six months.

Free Cash Rebate Programs

What's better than paying off your student loans a few months or years early by adding a few bucks to your payments? How about getting free money to pay off your student loans through shopping and credit card reward programs?

Shopping programs come in two forms: general cash rebate programs and student loan–specific cash rebate programs. Most cash rebate programs you find online will offer you a percentage of what you spend on shopping online for clothes, electronics, travel bookings, sports equipment, and more. Others will allow rebates for restaurants and even mortgages. Student loan rebate programs may even deposit the money directly into your student loan account.

Whichever program you choose to use, check their record on the Better Business Bureau Web site (www.bbb.org) to make sure the company you are thinking about choosing has few or no customer complaints.

Debunking Rewards Programs Myths

Upromise by Sallie Mae's Debby Hohler shows you how you can get money toward paying off your student loans without spending a dime beyond your regular budget.

Myth: Upromise is only for helping families save for college.

Fact: While you can use rewards earned through the Upromise program toward saving for your child's education, you can use it to pay down your student loans as well.

Myth: You have to buy extra things that you don't need in order to rack up Upromise rewards.

Fact: You can spend the same amount you normally would, but by shopping participating merchants you can collect meaningful money back for your student loans. Michelle, a Upromise member with over $35,000 in student loan debt, used her Upromise account only to buy things she was going to purchase anyway.

She earned Upromise savings when booking business travel. She uses the grocery coupons that she prints form the Upromise Web site to earn more rewards. She also faxes the coupon list to her dad so he can purchase these items and earn rewards for her as well. Her boyfriend earns Upromise savings for her when he shops online. She also got 25 percent of her electric bill back in rewards from her electric carrier for choosing a plan that includes green energy.

Without any excessive spending, she earned $315 this year to put toward her student loans. How much could $315 per year save someone in time to pay off her loans if she had $40,000 in educational debt at a 4 percent interest rate? On a 10-year plan, the time savings would be eight months. On a 25-year payment plan, the time savings would be four years and two months.

Myth: You can only earn Upromise rewards for online purchases.

Fact: Through Upromise dining partners you can earn rewards as high as 8 percent when you go out to eat, and you can earn rewards on everything you do through the Upromise credit card. You can even get rewards when you buy or sell a home and many other ways as well.

Myth: You have to have Sallie Mae loans to be a Upromise member.

Fact: Upromise offers Sallie Mae borrowers the ability to automatically transfer money to their student loan account on a quarterly basis, but anyone can get a check every quarter for the sum of their rewards that they can use to make a payment toward their student loans.

Bottom line: Free money is good money. You can take advantage of these kinds of programs to pay off your loans faster without spending anything beyond what you would normally spend.

Credit Card Rewards

If your credit card offers a cash-back program, you could be earning cash right now that you could save up to make extra payments on your student loans. But there are major cautions and considerations when it comes to using credit cards for rewards:

- Only charge what you can reasonably pay off in the same month.

- Even if you pay off your credit cards in the same month, your credit score recognizes what your highest balance was for the month. Unless you are charging on your card for an actual emergency, always stay under 15 percent of your limit.

- Compare rates and cash-back programs among at least three credit cards. These could be three that you already have or three new ones you've found through research. Look at what the interest rate is if you plan on leaving charges on for more than a month. Find out if there is an annual fee, and how many cash-back rewards can be earned. For example, cards may have different limits on how much of your charges can earn cash back. There could also be special bonus cash-back rewards for special purchases such as for gas and groceries. Compare offers before applying for new credit cards.

- Ask your bank about other rewards programs it might offer. Your bank may have a great rewards program you could switch to right now, and all it takes is one phone call.

Checklist for Rewards Programs

✓ Free money for online shopping is great as long you don't increase your spending to gain more cash-back savings.

✓ Only sign up for rewards programs associated with credit cards or Web sites that have good Better Business Bureau ratings.

✓ Don't put your finances in jeopardy by over-utilizing credit card rewards programs at the risk of blowing your budget.

✓ Don't charge more than 15 percent of your limit—even if you plan on paying off your debt at the end of the month.

Government Programs

While the government isn't going to repay your loans at record speed, there are government programs for loan forgiveness based on working for the government, income-based payment, and more that will help you repay some or all of your loans at least five years faster than consolidation alone. For more details, check out Chapter 2.

Using Online Calculators

Want to know how much your extra payment or direct debit interest rate deduction will help you in the long run? Use online calculators. Online financial calculators abound across the Internet. You can most likely find a few on your bank's Web site, among countless other sites. You can calculate how fast an interest rate decrease will help you pay off your student loans, as well as an extra payment. Graduates returning to school can use online calculators to compute future student loan payments.

You can also input balance transfer fees along with interest rates to compare credit card transfer offers. And when you're ready to buy a home, you can compare mortgages and refinancing deals.

Online calculators are easier to use than any calculator you've used in your entire life. You just input what you know about your loan and leave the input blank for what you want to know.

There are only two things you need to be aware of:

- **Each online calculator has a unique purpose.** Find a calculator that will solve what you need solved, such as one that compares mortgage offers or evaluates extra payments.

- **Ask for help when you need it**. If you still have questions, ask your loan servicer or contact the Web site. While using online calculators is easy, the results can be tricky. For example, calculating payments and payoff times for private loans is difficult when you have a variable interest rate, because you can't predict what your interest rate will be years down the line.

Online calculators are one tool for helping you with your finances. Use the information you find as part of your decision-making process, but also have your loan servicer double-check the results for you.

Checklist for Using Online Calculators

✓ Use online calculators to figure out how much an extra payment or interest rate decrease will benefit you.

✓ Find online calculators by searching on the Internet or on your bank or loan servicer's Web site.

✓ Before inputting the numbers you know, make sure the calculator you choose is specifically for gathering the information you want.

✓ Have your loan servicer double-check the numbers for you.

Chapter Wrap-Up

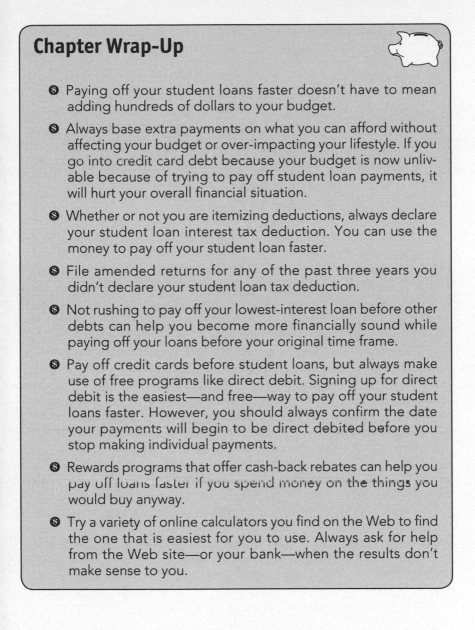

- Ⓢ Paying off your student loans faster doesn't have to mean adding hundreds of dollars to your budget.

- Ⓢ Always base extra payments on what you can afford without affecting your budget or over-impacting your lifestyle. If you go into credit card debt because your budget is now unlivable because of trying to pay off student loan payments, it will hurt your overall financial situation.

- Ⓢ Whether or not you are itemizing deductions, always declare your student loan interest tax deduction. You can use the money to pay off your student loan faster.

- Ⓢ File amended returns for any of the past three years you didn't declare your student loan tax deduction.

- Ⓢ Not rushing to pay off your lowest-interest loan before other debts can help you become more financially sound while paying off your loans before your original time frame.

- Ⓢ Pay off credit cards before student loans, but always make use of free programs like direct debit. Signing up for direct debit is the easiest—and free—way to pay off your student loans faster. However, you should always confirm the date your payments will begin to be direct debited before you stop making individual payments.

- Ⓢ Rewards programs that offer cash-back rebates can help you pay off loans faster if you spend money on the things you would buy anyway.

- Ⓢ Try a variety of online calculators you find on the Web to find the one that is easiest for you to use. Always ask for help from the Web site—or your bank—when the results don't make sense to you.

Reaping the Rewards of a Frugal Lifestyle

Remember that really horrible diet you tried that required flexing all of your discipline muscles at once? Well, just like an all-cabbage diet can only last so long before you quit and gain the weight back—plus a few extra pounds—an all-sacrifice financial diet eventually leads to unbridled spending as an act of rebellion where you recharge all your credit card debt—plus a few bonus charges you hadn't previously thought to make.

A reward system where you can splurge a little is part of any good diet, financial or otherwise. The trick in either realm is to make sure the rest of your diet isn't junk food or junk expenses.

Those of us with large amounts of student loan debt can't live on paying off student loan debt alone. We need to have some fun, too. We can buy the items we want, go out for drinks, and take an occasional vacation—and still stay within our budget.

We can do this by grouping rewards based on the expense, from eating out to saving for a new car to getting the house we crave. While dining out with coupon in tow is something we can work into our budget immediately, we can look forward to saving for retirement, buying a home, and living a great, financially balanced lifestyle.

How to Budget for Fun Extras

You have your financial diet down to a tee, and you worked in your personal must-haves in Chapter 5, "Budgeting for Your Lifestyle and Your Loans." You haven't gone one martini beyond your budget. But beyond what you allow yourself every month, you can now begin to save for reward items.

Small rewards may mean a bonus gourmet coffee after a month of staying on budget, a night out with friends, a pedicure, or forgetting about your gas budget for the day and taking a long drive.

How do you get started on the fun side of savings? Start a fun account. This can be earmarked within your regular checking or savings account or as a separate account. I prefer a separate account because then you can see the money you are putting aside for fun extras. I have a goal-orientated account for fun extras into which I deposit a few dollars a week. I don't want to spend the money until I get enough for the bicycle I want. In order to not tempt myself to withdraw money before my goal is reached, my fun account doesn't have an ATM card.

The amount you put in your fun extras account depends on your monthly budget. For example, if you already have 10 percent a month going into your savings account to build your emergency fund, and you have $200 left over at the end of the of the month, you could put $100 a month into your short-term fun extras account and $100 into your long-term fun extras account. How you distribute your fun money is up to you.

Link short-term fun accounts to your checking account but not your long-term fun account. Your long-range account should be at a different bank, so it's not as easy to access the money. This is a good idea for your emergency savings, too. If it's not at your normal bank, especially linked to your checking account, you won't be tempted to grab money out of it for a got-to-have-this-item-now moment. For emergency savings, you still want the bank to be pretty close to your home, maybe a few miles away. This way your cash isn't impossible to get to if you need it.

Fun-Account Strategies

Your fun account contains a specified amount for extras that you don't count as personal must-haves in your budget (see Chapter 5 for more on budgeting for your personal must-haves). For example, you budget $80 a month for gourmet coffees, but you don't feel a manicure and pedicure are high enough priorities in your budget to become monthly expenses. This is where a fun account comes in for occasional splurges. You can splurge on whatever you want as long as it comes out of your short-term fun account.

But how do you get the cash to go into your short-term and long-term fun accounts? You can come up with the money for a fun account in several ways:

- **Work in miscellaneous fun as a budget item.** The amount you set aside should be no more than half of the remaining amount you have in your budget after all of your other expenses are deducted. For example, if you bring home $2,500 a month and you have $2,200 earmarked for budget items, you can add another $150 to your emergency savings account, investments, or to pay down your credit cards. Then budget the remaining $150 for miscellaneous fun.

- **At the end of the month, find areas of your budget where you didn't spend the full amount you allowed yourself.** For example, if you budget $80 a month for coffees, and you only spent $40, the remaining $40 can go into your fun account. Just don't take the extra money from an expense like electricity or your gas bill that can vary from month to month. Leaving the money in your checking account will help you cover the electric bill for a month when there's a heat wave and you use more air conditioning than normal. This way you have a checking account safety net to make sure you are never overdrawn.

- **Save reward splurges for fun accounts.** Going shopping because you lost weight, improved your credit score, or remembered to call your mom on Mother's Day depletes your account. Especially if you reward yourself often with purchases, you could start to build up credit card debt or make emergency savings impossible. Instead, celebrate life's milestones by adding money to your fun account at the end of the month. Then the next time you want to make a purchase dedicated to an accomplishment, the money will be waiting for you in your fun account.

- **Overtime.** Ideally, you don't want to work overtime in order to afford your monthly expenses. However, working occasional overtime to put money into a fun account doesn't feel like you're giving up your free time to work. Instead, you're working to make your free time more pleasurable. Just don't work so much that you don't have time to spend any of the money in your fun account.

- **Bonuses or promotions.** When you get a big bonus at work or a promotion, your first thought might be to spend, spend, spend. But if you put a portion of that money in your savings account or toward paying down your debts, then you can add the rest to your fun account and not feel guilty.

Checklist for Funding a Fun Account

✓ Have a method for how you acquire your fun account money, such as putting away half of any unused money from your budget, part of bonuses or promotion money, or by including fun accounts as a budgeting item.

✓ Keep short- and long-term fun accounts separate. You'll find it easier to save for vacations if your small splurges don't come out of the same fun account.

✓ Watch linking fun accounts to your checking account. Doing so makes it extra easy to withdraw money and deplete your fun experiences.

✓ Always have general goals for your long-term account. You don't want to save for a vacation and then not have the money when you're ready to use it because you dipped into that account for nights out.

Stretching Your Fun Account Further

Congratulations on setting up a fun account! By thinking through your splurges, you can make your fun dollars go even further.

Don't Be a Sucker for Sales

Who doesn't love a good sale, with 25 percent or more off clothes, household décor, video games, and MP3 players, or spa days that are on special? But when you walk in planning to spend $50 on a video game and you walk out with five video games—or you walk in for a haircut and walk out having enjoyed a hot-stone massage, aromatherapy, pedicure, European facial, sea-salt scrub, *and* a haircut—you may have saved $100 off what these items would normally cost due to sale prices, but do you feel good about spending $200 more than what you intended?

Sale-Daze Spending Exercise

Overbuying sale items can result in buying items you don't want, need, or can't afford. In this exercise, you'll determine how much you could have saved by not getting sucked in by sale prices. Fill in the chart with the items you bought solely because they were on sale over the last four months. Estimate item prices you don't remember.

What Did You Buy?	How Much Did It Cost?	How Many Times Was It Used?	Do You Still Use It?
Total:			

Now, subtract from your total the amount of the items you purchased, the total price of the items you listed that you are still happy you bought. This is the total of your sales waste.

Checklist for Sale Control

✓ Your fun account will go further if you are careful to avoid sale daze.

✓ Review your chart to determine if there are items you wouldn't have bought if you could remake your decision.

✓ Before buying additional items just because they are on sale, think about whether you will use the item, and whether you'd be better off spending the money elsewhere.

Eating Out

Have you ever gone into a restaurant thinking you were going to spend under $40 for dinner and ended up with a bill for $100? I have. My friends and I start by picking out $10 to $15 entrées. Then we check out the appetizer portion of the menu and decide we must have jalapeño poppers, which adds $10 to the bill. Then we order salads because they don't come with the entrée, thus adding another $3 each to our meal. Then there are drinks, a dessert to split, tax, and tip. We walk out very full—and with a doggie bag to boot—but we spend over twice what we had planned.

If this scenario sounds familiar, know that overspending on dining is easily avoidable if you keep in mind three different strategies.

ONLINE MENUS

Looking at menus online before you go out puts you in total control of your spending situation. View the menu ahead of time, pick what you want to order, and add up the total costs. As a bonus, you can increase your odds of your waiter or waitress getting your order right by writing down what you pick and handing it to your server at the restaurant.

But doesn't this strategy take the spontaneity out of going out, you might ask? Picking your food from an online menu can actually increase spontaneity, because instead of just going to the same restaurant you always choose, you can browse the Internet and find a restaurant in your neighborhood you've never tried. You can savor exotic dishes you wouldn't normally order. Would you rather get into the same predicament I did, and spend over twice as much as you intended? That extra $60 amounts to 12 extra coffees, a month's cable bill, four movie nights, or two comedy club visits.

ONLINE COUPONS

Clipping coupons isn't how it used to be: You no longer have to scour just the newspaper fliers. You can go online and search for restaurant coupons in your city or in your favorite vacation spot. In addition to online versions of what you could find in print, there are numerous sites offering printable coupons that save you money. For example, www.restaurant.com offers $10, $25, and $50 gift certificates for thousands of restaurants across the country for $3, $10, and $20, respectively. You can normally find additional discount codes by signing up on www.restaurant.com, or do a simple Web search for www.restaurant.com promo codes to reduce the price even further.

Saving Money While Dining Out

Tony Bombacino of www.restaurant.com gives you the facts on saving money when eating out.

Myth: If you use coupons or gift certificates when dining out, you'll look cheap in front of your friends, your dates, or your significant other.

Fact: You're actually considered savvy and can afford more great meals while you pay off your loans and live your life. There's an upward momentum of educated buyers whose coupon and gift certificate use increases year after year. Your buddies will be more likely to ask you where you got your coupons, instead of why are you using one.

Myth: Tips for servers can be discounted at the same rate as the total bill when you are using restaurant coupons or discounted gift certificates.

Fact: Servers earn most of their restaurant wages from gratuity. When using a restaurant gift certificate, be kind to your server. Calculate the tip based on what the bill would have cost without the gift certificate or coupon and show your appreciation.

Myth: Budgeting means giving up dining out.

Fact: You can do both. You can in fact go out to eat more often when you buy www.restaurant.com $25 restaurant gift certificates for as little as $2 (during an 80 percent off promotion), or for $10 when no promotion is running. Have your cake, sushi, steak, cheesecake, or whatever you like, and afford it too.

TAKEOUT AND DELIVERY

Want a romantic dinner with a controlled cost structure? Order delivery, set the table, and light candles before your dinner arrives. You can order far more than Chinese takeout and pizza in most cities.

Search the Internet to find a restaurant that delivers in your area. When you go out to eat, ask the restaurant if it delivers as well. They may not, but there are also services that will charge fees from $5 to $15 to deliver to your home. However, you'll still save money because you won't be tempted to buy drinks, appetizers, and desserts that can double or even triple your final bill.

Checklist for Eating Out

✓ Eating out can be part of your budget, as long as you pay attention to the amount you spend.

✓ Reviewing online menus can not only help you budget better, but can lead to eating at restaurants you might normally not try.

✓ Use online coupons. You could eat out for half the normal price.

✓ Any delivery charges can be easily made up by the drinks, appetizers, and desserts you are less likely to order when you are getting food delivered.

Saving on Vacations

It's tax return time and everyone and their brother is telling you to take a fabulous trip with them. It may be a cruise to the Caribbean, a shopping and/or clubbing weekend in New York, island hopping in Hawaii, or rafting in Costa Rica. But can you afford it, and what will it do to your finances for the rest of the year?

Before you plan for a vacation—or set aside the fun money to splurge in case the perfect trip arises at the last moment—look at your budget and check your fun account balance.

If you are planning a vacation in advance, you have time to research the best deals, find off-peak specials (specials for traveling during less popular times), and build up spending money to thoroughly enjoy your trip.

AFFORDING LAST-MINUTE VACATIONS

Last-minute vacations are still possible with a little budgeting elbow grease. Here's what you need to consider when deciding whether to take a last-minute trip:

- **Are your bills in good order?** You never want to take a trip at the expense of paying your bills. You can always take a fabulous vacation later, when you're in better shape financially.

- **Are your credit cards paid off?** It's a vacation in itself when you don't have to worry about making payments on your credit cards. Think about how close that money you're considering putting toward a vacation would get you toward freeing yourself from credit card debt.

- **Do you have an exact tally on the cost of the trip?** Everything requires a budget—even last-minute trips. Have you thought about food, entertainment, trinkets, evenings out, hotels, and flights? Have you priced out these items based on realistic estimates from the area to which you want to travel? If you haven't, it's a good idea to contact a hotel concierge, look at city guides, and view online sites for restaurants and tourist attractions.

- **Have you planned for emergency money?** In addition to what the actual vacation costs, do you have extra money if you lose your passport and have to get a new one, or your vacation expenses are slightly more than you planned on?

OFF-SEASON VACATIONS

Resorts often have different rates for going in off-season and peak-season times. Traveling in the off season could be half the cost. But will it be half the fun?

Have your parents ever taken you to a theme park on a day when it was a little chilly or there was a possibility of rain? Mine have. We didn't have to wait in any lines, and we were able to ride everything at least three times.

Off-season vacations can mean getting your own near-private island. In a past relationship, I went to Catalina Island in the off season and paid less than half of the peak-season rates for a junior suite. With only 220 tourists on the whole island, we had the place pretty much to ourselves. We hiked through the hills and walked along the beach. There was only one other couple on the tour we took through the mountains. We were able to sit at a café sipping wine while chatting with locals. Dinner reservations were made with an hour's notice.

This doesn't mean there weren't sacrifices, though. The water would have been cold if you wanted to go kayaking in January, but for us, the private island feel more than made up for a chilly ocean.

> ### Caution
>
> Make sure "off season" does not mean hurricane season! Do some research before you make reservations. Traveling off season can be fabulous, but you don't want your vacation turning into a natural disaster.

TIPS FOR SAVVY VACATION PLANNING

Whether your vacation is last minute or booked a year in advance, these tips will keep your trip from being a budget buster:

- **Pick your splurges carefully.** Everyone has their own vacation style. For some, eating the best of local cuisine takes the highest priority. For others, it's having an adventure. Prioritize what's important to you for each day of your vacation and spend accordingly.

- **Make any vacation all-inclusive.** All-inclusive resorts and cruises with food, entertainment, and lodging are great for budgeting. But you can make any vacation into a nearly all-inclusive event by planning the details ahead of time. For example, you set an amount you want to spend for your weekend getaway, such as $500. You choose a bed and breakfast for $140 per night, including tax, which includes breakfast and evening cocktails. That leaves you $220 for activities and food. You can pay for activities and tips ahead of time online, where you also found the best deals. Then you just use the remainder for food.

- **Look for hotel packages.** Many hotels offer theme packages such as shopping, girls' or guys' weekends, or romance. Extras might include dinner, champagne, massages, nightclub passes, and more. Sometimes the packages are cheaper than the room by itself. Always look for these packages on the hotel's official Web site, or ask about it when you call for reservations.

- **Don't rule out places by distance.** You may be able to fly to a place that has inexpensive hotels and activities instead of living it up closer to home. For example, you might fly to New Zealand and get a hotel, travel, and touring package for six nights for around $1,600. But if you fly to New York or San Francisco where the hotel you want to stay in is $1,200 for the week, without any activities or airfare, it might be cheaper to vacation in New Zealand.

- **Be flexible with flight dates.** If one flight is less full than another, you may get a better deal because airlines need to fill seats. Click "flexible dates" when booking online or tell the phone reservation agent that your travel dates are flexible. You could find a cheaper flight one day before or after when you were planning on leaving.

- **Vacation at home.** Take an inexpensive "staycation"—read a book, go on a picnic, or enjoy a local museum. Or you can create a relaxing home environment all year long—and save money at the same time—by purchasing a few luxury items: a cappuccino machine for drinking your morning coffee at home, a home facial kit for fewer days spent at the spa, or a vacuuming robot to cut down on using a cleaning service.

BUDGETING DAILY FOR A WEEK-LONG VACATION

You're lying by the pool next to your best friend. The server comes by and asks you if you want another drink. You don't blink before saying, yes—or signing the room charge slip. Later in the day you stop by the concierge to figure out what you want to do next. Parasailing sounds perfect, and you sign another slip. What's another signature when you planned on $1,000 in spending money for your vacation? By the end of the week, though, you've managed to rack up $1,900 in charges on your credit card. And unless you get a cash advance on your card, you won't be able to pay your rent on time.

What happened?

You thought about your vacation with a seemingly endless budget. Instead, you should have thought about your vacation as seven individual days, each with activities and expenses.

Constructing a daily budget forces you to think about all the activities and meals you want to have on your vacation. For instance, you can look at the restaurant menus at your hotel and approximate what you want to eat for a certain day. This may change depending on outdoor activities you may choose, like kayaking, where you'll buy a $10 bagged lunch from your hotel.

Constructing daily budgets also forces you to think about coupons you wouldn't normally think about once your mind has switched over to "vacation mode." In vacation-mode thinking, life is breezy. Your bills are miles away, and you are thinking about the next way to unwind. This is a version of I-deserve-it mode when you buy clothing, electronics, or a new car because of a workplace promotion—although you still have $10,000 in credit card debt from when you weren't making as much money.

The next time you consider taking a vacation, construct a daily budget using the following format. Leave a few lines for each day, since you will likely want to eat more than once a day and do more than one activity. Don't worry about sticking to exactly what you write down, it's just a guideline. Substitute other activities you might like to do if others seem dull or unnecessary when you arrive.

For the rows, write Day 1 through Day 7. For the columns, you might list the following:

- Activities
- Hotel and airfare (list the full amounts for the trip on day one)
- Food
- Shopping
- Ground transportation
- Spontaneity (unplanned expenses)

You deserve the best vacation you can afford without feeling like you're on the anti-vacation when you return to a larger pile of credit card debt and a landlord tapping his heels at your doorstep. Just don't let your other bills slide in order to take the perfect vacation.

Checklist for Vacations

✓ Avoid traveling during the peak seasons when possible.

✓ Check room charges daily. Signing room charge slips repeatedly can lead to forgetting what you're spending.

✓ Whether it's cruises, resorts, plane tickets, or activities, do your research to find the best deals.

✓ Have everything planned out ahead of time, and look for online coupons and deals.

✓ Set aside a few dollars for spontaneity and unplanned expenses.

You've Earned a New Car

You just landed a job in a company where it seems that every other car in the parking garage shines with status, while your car glimmers with "I still haven't replaced my college vehicle." You want to fit in now, but you're not sure your budget can handle it.

First, research the cars you are considering by looking at both user reviews on the Internet and maintenance and performance reviews from car blogs and magazine Web sites.

Test-drive the car you are most interested in or call rental agencies to see if you can rent the same make and model of what you're thinking about purchasing. Renting a car for a couple of days is a great way to get an idea of how much you'd enjoy driving it on a regular basis.

Once you've narrowed down your search to two or three cars, price your future ride. Find out how much the car payment would be by going to the car company Web sites and building and pricing the vehicle you'd like to have. Then go to the financing pages of the Web sites to calculate your monthly payment. Pick a time frame that is shorter than how long you plan on keeping your car. It's fine to pick a five-year payment plan if you plan on keeping the car for seven years. But if you plan on trading your vehicle in after five years, you should pick a three- or four-year payment plan.

Write down the payment amount, then call your car insurance company and find out how much the car you want to buy would cost to insure with full coverage. Add the cost of your insurance to your prospective car payment. This is the number you use for budgeting. Make this payment into your long-range savings account for six months. If you can spare the money from your checking account for this period of time, you can likely afford to buy the car. Plus, you have six months to think about whether your employment is stable and if you have other goals you'd rather spend the money on.

Once you've decided you definitely want to buy a new vehicle, compare the price and the loan terms among at least three different dealerships. Do not buy anything until you've done this. If you budget and compare prices carefully, you can end up with a car you love—and more importantly, can afford—for the best deal possible.

Checklist for Saving for a Car

✓ Research the best car payments and prices via the Internet.

✓ Test-drive the cars you are interested in.

✓ Read reviews about maintenance and performance.

✓ Add the cost of car insurance to your prospective car payment.

✓ Practice saving for a car payment for six months.

✓ Compare price and loan terms of at least three dealers.

Moving into a Nicer Place

Your studio apartment is starting to feel smaller and smaller. You'd love to lease an apartment or condo uptown that's closer to work and has its own gym. Your goal could also be to buy your own spacious house in the 'burbs.

Have your dreams outpaced your bank account?

There's only one way to find out where you can afford to live. Calculate the total expenses of your new home compared to where you are. Then pre-budget for the difference, and save for initial and incidental expenses attached to your new locale.

What expenses do you need to include?

If you want to buy a home, consider all the expenses you currently have, including utilities, transportation, cable, and phone. Then add home maintenance, homeowners association fees, and homeowner's insurance. This is what you could pay if your new mortgage was the same amount as your current rent.

If you are renting, you'll mainly want to look at differences, such as additional electricity charges if you are moving to a larger place or parking fees if your current place doesn't charge for parking.

To get an accurate reading of what your electricity bill will cost in the new places you are considering, ask the leasing agent, the local utility company, or your real estate agent. Approximations are available based on the electric usage of past residents.

Then take all the information you've gathered and create a chart to compare expenses. For the rows, use housing cost categories such as transportation, utilities, rent, and homeowner's or renter's insurance. For the columns, list your current home, housing choice 1, housing choice 2, and housing choice 3. (Whether it's homes, apartments, car dealers, or cell phone companies, you should always compare at least three options before making a decision.)

If you are creating the chart by hand in your notebook, leave several lines between each row representing a housing choice.

When you are considering buying a home, in addition to planning for your monthly budget, start putting savings into your fun account for your down payment and emergencies. For the exact amount you should put aside for your down payment, consult a loan officer at your bank; he can tell you about how your credit rating or debt payments compared to income might affect how much you need to have available. Ideally, 20 percent of the home price is optimal for a down payment, but 10 percent is a great goal.

For the amount you should have available at all times for emergencies, you should put away at least six months' worth of your bare-bones budget. This is because when you have a home, you can't just sign another lease for a lower-rent apartment whenever you can't afford your payment.

Refer to Chapter 5 for tips on negotiating housing prices. After all, if you can negotiate a lower price, you may be able to afford a whole lot more in a rental or purchased home on the same budget.

Checklist for Movin' Up and Movin' On

✓ Compare the difference in costs between where you are currently living to where you would like to live.

✓ Do enough research to come up with an educated estimate of what your new place will cost.

✓ Always compare at least three places, so you know you are getting the best deal.

Feeling Financially Secure

The best reward you can gather from completing the regular and fun account budgeting exercises is feeling financially secure: not sweating when your student loan payment is due, not worrying that a check might bounce, and being able to fund your 401k account up to the amount your employer will match. Rewarding yourself for living within a personalized budget is key to achieving your goal of managing your student debt over the long haul.

Chapter Wrap-Up

- Budgeting doesn't mean going on a financial fast from fun. Save a few dollars in a fun account so you can reward yourself with extras.

- Have a methodology for how your fun money is derived and stick with it.

- Have goals. A budget that doesn't help you toward where you want to be in the future is barely worth having. Always think of your fun expenses on the grand scale of where you want to be six months, one year, or five years down the line.

- Having goal-orientated accounts divided by whether you are saving for small or large splurges will help you to both prioritize and not take out the money you want for your down payment on your first home to pay for a new set of luggage.

- Don't spend excessively on sale items. No matter what the price is, if you buy an item on sale that you will never use, you're still wasting money.

- The best way to curtail restaurant spending is to plan what you're going to spend and stick with it.

- Plan your vacations in advance based on daily budgets for expenses. You'll find great deals on activities by conducting research on the Internet.

- Don't buy a car until you've practiced making payments for at least six months. It's better to find out now if you can't afford a car payment instead of when it's repossessed.

- Your debt won't go away tomorrow, so have fun in the meantime. Depriving yourself will eventually cause a splurge that will get you back to feeling trapped by your debt.

Index